PRUNING
Simplified

PRUNING
Simplified

A VISUAL GUIDE TO 50 TREES AND SHRUBS

STEVEN BRADLEY

TIMBER PRESS

A QUARTO BOOK

This edition published in 2019
by Timber Press, Inc.
The Haseltine Building
133 S.W. Second Avenue, Suite 450
Portland, Oregon 97204-3527
timberpress.com

ISBN: 978-1-60469-888-6

A catalog record for this book is
available from the Library of Congress.

Conceived, edited, and designed by
Quarto Publishing
an imprint of The Quarto Group
The Old Brewery
6 Blundell Street
London N7 9BH
www.quartoknows.com

QUAR: AVGP

Publisher's note
Some gardening tasks can be hazardous,
especially when using powered tools.
Always exercise caution. Read the
instruction manuals and follow the safety
guidance provided. As far as the methods
and techniques mentioned in this book are
concerned, all statements, information,
and advice given here are believed to be
true and accurate. However, neither the
author, copyright holder, nor the publisher
can accept any legal liability for
errors or omissions.

Printed in China

CONTENTS

WHY PRUNE?

At its simplest, pruning is a means of manipulating a plant's growth, shape, and productivity by cutting and training it to achieve what you want to happen. To prune plants well is not so much about knowing how and where to cut but about knowing what you are trying to achieve.

The main reasons for pruning are to train a plant to grow in a particular way, to balance its growth, to control the production of flowers and fruit, to maintain its health, and to restrict its growth. A final type of pruning, remedial or renovation pruning, may also be necessary from time to time.

TRAINING

Careful pruning in the early years—often referred to as formative pruning—will allow you to create a plant that is well-proportioned, attractive, and that carries flowers or fruits where they are visible and easily reached for picking. A tree or shrub with well-spaced stems and branches with good angles will reduce the risk of breakage and stem splitting. Plants pruned correctly while they are young are easier to care for in later years. Time spent on training and pruning young plants should be regarded as an investment in their future and as a time-saving, long-term benefit for the gardener.

BALANCING GROWTH

A healthy plant should show signs of vigorous, active growth, especially when it is young and establishing itself. Most plants will start to flower earlier in their lives if they are allowed to grow naturally. Young woody plants will often produce only a few flowers until they are established. As plants mature and begin to flower and fruit on a regular basis, the production of shoots will slow down, with fewer and shorter new shoots being produced each year. As plants age, there is less annual growth. While leaves are produced on older and on younger wood, it is often the younger wood that produces the flowers.

From the gardener's point of view, it is important that a plant's shoot growth and flower production are going on at the same time. Pruning should strike a balance, allowing woody plants to continue producing young woody stems while providing a regular display of flowers and fruits. Often, the timing of pruning can maintain this balance. Pruning plants in late winter and early spring, for example, often encourages the plant to produce lots of new shoots, whereas pruning in midsummer can induce a plant to produce more flower or fruit buds for the following year. Removing old flowerheads (deadheading) to prevent plants from producing seeds will help to extend the flowering season if their energy is not devoted to producing seeds.

Well-pruned plants will produce more flowers, more fruit, or more colorful stems or leaves.

About this book

The introductory section (pages 6–15) outlines the essential reasons for pruning, with information on tools and equipment, health and safety, and basic pruning techniques. The main part of the book is the plant directory (pages 16–151), which features over 50 of the most widely grown garden plants. Arranged alphabetically by botanical name, each entry includes detailed pruning instructions and illustrations specific to each plant. After the directory (pages 152–183), you will find articles on specialist pruning topics, such as hedges, groundcover, and climbers. In addition, at the back of the book are some tables giving at-a-glance summaries of information, including a list of no- or low-prune plants, and a glossary.

Satellite diagrams and subsidiary illustrations identify key techniques.

Pruning points are clearly marked and explained in a key at the bottom of the page.

Botanical name

Common name(s)

Identification photograph of a popular species or cultivar

How pruning will benefit this plant

Handy pruning tips for the plant

When to prune the majority of the plant's species and cultivars. This does not refer to all species and cultivars; if you are unsure, refer to your local nursery.

List of the most widely grown plants that are pruned in the same manner. Although the techniques are similar, pruning times may differ and so these are provided for each plant.

Necessary pruning tools and equipment

Clear step-by-step pruning instructions, organized into formative, routine, and remedial pruning

Detailed illustration demonstrates the routine pruning of the plant. The dulled sections of the illustration indicate stems or parts of stems to be pruned.

26 DIRECTORY OF PLANTS

BERBERIS
(deciduous species)
Berberis, barberry

Berberis are good-value shrubs, providing leaf color, flowers, and berries, even in unpromising conditions.

WHY PRUNE?
To make sure that a supply of new shoots emerges from ground level each year.

PRUNING TIPS
Wait until summer to remove dead wood—it is much easier to see then.

WHEN TO PRUNE MOST SPECIES
Early summer

PLANTS PRUNED THIS WAY
• *Berberis ×ottawensis*, in early summer, immediately after flowering
• *Berberis ×rubrostilla*, in early summer, immediately after flowering
• *Berberis thunbergii*, in early summer, immediately after flowering
• *Berberis wilsoniae*, in early summer, immediately after flowering

WHICH TOOLS
• Hand pruners
• Long-handled pruners (loppers)
• Thornproof leather gloves

FORMATIVE PRUNING
Prune young plants to encourage them to develop a bushy habit with strong shoots emerging from ground level. After planting, cut out any weak or damaged growth. Lightly pinch back the remaining shoots to about two-thirds of their length so that the plant will form new shoots from the base.

ROUTINE PRUNING
If they are to flower well, berberis need regular annual pruning to remove a proportion of the old wood and to encourage new flower-bearing shoots. Also, if you have a plant with purple or variegated leaves you should prune so that young shoots, which tend to have more attractive color, replace old ones. Immediately after flowering in early summer, cut the old flower-bearing stems back to a strong pair of buds or to lower, younger shoots. This will eliminate the fruits, which can be spread easily by birds, and will give the maximum period of growth to produce a good display of flowers the following year. On mature shrubs try to remove between one-quarter and one-fifth of the old stems each year to allow light in and to make room for new shoots.

REMEDIAL PRUNING
Berberis tend to form a matted clump of branches, and the inner branches often shed their leaves and die from lack of light. Plants respond well to severe pruning. In early summer, remove all dead or weak shoots. Cut all healthy stems back to within 12in (30cm) of ground level.

GENERAL HABIT OF MATURE PLANT

Remedial pruning: Cut out old stems just above a replacement shoot.

Remove old stems.

= Routine pruning
Dead and defective growth

BERBERIS (DECIDUOUS) 27

Cut back to a healthy pair of buds.

CONTROLLING FLOWER AND FRUIT QUALITY

As plants develop a cycle of flowering and fruiting regularly, they often slip into overproduction. You have only to look at a rose or crabapple that has been left unpruned for a number of years to see that the more flowers and fruit a plant produces, the smaller they become. Often, too, the flowers and fruits on the inner sections of the branches are not only small but of poor quality.

Pruning away some sections of stems and branches allows you to remove some of the poorer stems altogether. Pruning weak stems also diverts energy into the production of larger, though fewer, flowers and fruit. A good example of this is the butterfly bush (*Buddleja davidii*). On an unpruned bush there may be profuse quantities of flower spikes, each about 4in (10cm) long. A plant that is pruned regularly and at the correct time of year, however, will bear a smaller number of flower spikes, but each may be 12in (30cm) or more long.

CREATING A PATTERN OF GROWTH

Some plants don't have particularly nice-looking flowers—in fact, some plants produce flowers that are barely noticeable—but other characteristics do make them attractive garden plants. A number of deciduous shrubs, including dogwoods (*Cornus* spp.) and willows (*Salix* spp.), have colored bark that is especially bright in winter, and other plants, such as some hazels (*Corylus* spp.) and elders (*Sambucus* spp.), have large, colorful leaves in spring and summer. These colored stems and large leaves are produced only from the current season's growth, and the more vigorous this growth is, the better the effect will be. In both instances, the vigorous growth can be achieved only by severe pruning, often cutting down whole plants to within 4–6in (10–15cm) of ground level each year.

Willows and dogwoods are often grown for their new growth, which provides beautiful color during the winter months. To achieve this, plants must be pruned hard annually.

MAINTAINING PLANT HEALTH

Combating pests and diseases is a vital part of gardening. Often the best method of control is prevention, either before a problem becomes established or even before it begins. Good pruning can preempt some serious problems, and good formative pruning to encourage strong stems and wide angles where branches join the main trunk will reduce the chance of branches splitting or breaking and providing a site where pests and diseases can take hold.

Many of the diseases that attack woody plants damage the wood and hence the whole structure of the plant. Disease often enters through dead tissue, such as a wound or injury, and is spread throughout the live, healthy parts of the plant. This is why the first part of any pruning process should be removing dead, dying, diseased, or damaged wood (the four Ds) before the real pruning begins.

Buddleia is an excellent choice for a garden shrub, but it must be pruned regularly to prevent it from smothering the surrounding plants and to encourage the production of larger, stronger shoots and bigger, more attractive flower spikes.

If there is any suspicion of disease, look for telltale signs, such as a brown staining in the wood on or just under the bark. Always cut back to healthy sections of branch or stem where there is no staining. Pruning to create a good, open structure will allow a free flow of air around the branches. This reduces the chance of diseases, including mildew, and helps to reduce hospitable areas for pests such as aphids that find shelter and become established in weakened and sheltered sites on plants.

Simply changing the time of year that you prune your plants can combat certain diseases. Oak wilt can kill strong, healthy oaks within a few years if it gains a foothold. The beetles that carry the oak wilt disease are active from late April through June in most parts of the country, so it is best to prune oaks in winter, when the beetles are not active. Cutting down tall roses to half their

height in an exposed garden will prevent them from rocking in the wind and suffering root damage through the winter.

RESTRICTING GROWTH

Perhaps the ultimate example of restrictive pruning is the practice of bonsai, but in a garden the most common use of clipping and pruning is to make rows of plants form a dense shelter or screen—a hedge.

Many plants will keep getting larger if they are left to develop naturally. In gardens and along pathways this can be a problem if space is restricted. In a natural setting it is often survival of the fittest and biggest, so large plants often crowd out smaller ones. Most gardeners face this at some stage and need to prune routinely to keep plants within their allotted area as well as encourage balanced growth and production of flowers and fruit.

REMEDIAL PRUNING

This type of pruning—often referred to as renovation pruning—is usually used to gain control of a plant that is not growing in a desirable way or one that has been neglected and becomes misshapen or unsightly. Remedial pruning varies in effectiveness. Some plants respond well and often recover, growing for many more years after getting a new lease on life. Unfortunately, other plants, such as brooms and many conifers, will not respond to this treatment and often die after severe pruning instead of regenerating themselves.

Even if plants respond positively, problems sometimes arise if they have been budded or grafted onto a rootstock (a healthy plant used as a root system for a grafted plant base), because the rootstock may grow as vigorously as the cultivar that has been grafted onto it. Also, if you are doing remedial pruning on a grafted plant, it is important to discover where the rootstock and scion (a young shoot from the desired plant) are joined together. If the plant is cut below this union, the cultivar will be removed and only sucker growth from the rootstock will emerge.

Remedial pruning can improve the plants in your garden, but don't expect miracles! Years of neglect cannot be rectified in one season.

Pruning is required to restrict the growth of plants alongside pathways or they can quickly take over the space.

EQUIPMENT

Pruning can be hard work, and it can be even more difficult if you have poor-quality or blunt tools that have not been regularly sharpened and oiled to stay in good condition.

HAND PRUNERS

Most pruning will be done with hand pruners, and the type you choose will be largely a matter of personal preference. There are two types of cutting mechanism:

- Anvil-type hand pruners have a single, straight-edged cutting blade that closes down onto an anvil, a bar of softer metal or plastic. Some have a ratchet mechanism for cutting through wood in stages, but this type of cutting action is slower than with conventional models. The anvil action is not ideal in some situations; it has a tendency to crush stems and split bark.
- Bypass hand pruners have cutting blades that pass one another and are the most popular pruning tool for small jobs. The scissor action makes a clean cut and will not splinter the branch edge.

LOPPERS AND LONG-ARM PRUNERS

- Long-handled pruners, often called loppers, are heavy-duty hand pruners for tackling thicker stems or branches. The long handles are for extra reach and leverage. They can have anvil or bypass cutting mechanisms.
- You can use long-arm pruners to prune high branches so that you don't need a ladder. They consist of a pole some 6–10ft (2–3m) long with a heavy-duty pruner at the tip. The blade is operated by pulling on a cable attached to the bottom of the pole. A model with shears fitted to the top is available for cutting high hedges.

Bypass hand pruners

Anvil-type hand pruners

Anvil-type hand pruners with ratchet mechanism

Long-handled bypass loppers

Long-handled anvil loppers

Long-arm pruners

SAWS

There are several types of pruning saws, which are used for cutting through larger branches:

- The Grecian saw is useful when branches are growing close together. It has a curved blade that tapers to a sharp point, and sloping teeth designed to cut on the pull stroke.
- Folding saws are a variation on the Grecian saw. They are designed to close with the blade setting into the handle—rather like a large pocket knife.
- Bow saws are fast-cutting and useful for sawing very thick branches (over 5in/13cm). They have a replaceable blade.
- Pole saws are used to prune high branches without a ladder. A pole, 6–10ft (2–3m) long, has a heavy-duty Grecian saw at the tip.

PRUNING KNIVES

Pruning knives have a curved blade that makes it easier for them to cut through thin stems and branches. The knife handle is usually fairly thick to provide extra grip.

SHEARS

Hand shears operate with a bypass cutting action and are used for cutting large volumes of thin, sappy material. Some models have a notch at the base of the blade for cutting thicker stems.

Grecian saw

Folding saw

Bow saw

Pruning knife

Hand shears

Leather gloves

Gauntlets

HEALTH AND SAFETY

- Tough leather gloves or gauntlets are a wise choice when pruning, especially when you are handling plants that have spines or thorns.
- If you have sensitive skin, wear gloves when pruning plants such as euphorbias, which exude an irritating sap, or rue (*Ruta* spp.), which can cause phytodermatitis, to avoid triggering an allergic reaction.
- It is often advisable to wear safety goggles or glasses, particularly when using powered tools or cutting implements. When you are engaged in jobs that are likely to create large amounts of dust or fumes, wear a face mask to protect your mouth and nose.
- When using garden machinery and tools, especially electric- or gasoline-driven items, always wear appropriate safety clothing, including gloves, ear and eye protectors, and sturdy footwear. Most machines have safety symbols to indicate the minimum protective clothing to be worn. Never wear loose, flapping clothing that could become caught in moving parts of machinery.
- Always drag large pieces of the debris you create as you prune clear of the area where you are working so that you don't get tangled in them and fall.
- Tools cannot function properly if they are dirty, rusty, or damaged. Clean all garden tools after using them.
- Take care if you decide to use a ladder when pruning. Always work from a supported stepladder or platform, and consider calling a professional, such as a landscaper or arborist, for pruning or removing large trees or heavy branches.

BASIC TECHNIQUES

To some extent you can determine the amount of basic pruning you will need to do by choosing good-quality plants that have no obvious signs of pests and diseases, damage, or injury and that are growing well (although that is not easy to tell during the dormant season).

When you are buying climbers, roses, and shrubs for your garden, select plants that have several healthy stems emerging from close to ground level. Trees with a vigorous single stem and sideshoots emerging at regular intervals almost at right angles to the main stem or trunk of the tree will form strong branches and a good framework as they mature.

MAKING A START

Before you prune any plant, it will help to have a basic idea of how that plant grows. You don't need to be a botanist, but you should have an idea of the plant's natural habit of

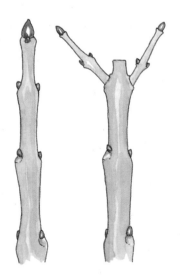

Plants with buds in opposite pairs will naturally produce a pair of shoots after the stem has been pruned.

growth—whether it should be erect, bushy, spreading, and so on—and when it flowers. This knowledge will give you some idea of the plant's likely reaction when you prune it, although you should bear in mind that most plants will react differently to pruning at different times of the year.

A quick examination of the plant you want to prune will show that at the tip of each shoot there is a terminal (apical) bud, which is often called the growing point. Below this bud on the stem are arranged other smaller side buds, called lateral (axillary) buds. These are arranged in a particular way, which varies from plant to plant. They get their name from the place where they form on the shoot—the leaf axil (or the angle where a leaf is attached to the stem of the plant). The position of these buds will determine where the future side (lateral) branches or flowering shoots are likely to develop.

The apical bud in the tip of the shoot influences the growth and development of the axillary buds by producing chemicals that discourage their growth, a characteristic known as apical dominance. If the apical bud is damaged or removed, its control is lost and the axillary buds or shoots respond by growing rapidly to form laterals or sideshoots.

Once they have reached their intended size, some plants will require only an annual trim with shears or a hedge trimmer.

Apical dominance seems to be much stronger in younger plants and is often more significant when plants are undergoing some type of formative pruning.

It is useful to understand how a plant will respond when you have to decide just where to make a pruning cut. Don't make the mistake of thinking that severe pruning is the best way to control vigorous growth in plants—in fact, severe pruning usually provokes the plant to grow even more vigorously.

POSITIONING PRUNING CUTS

On most of the plants you are likely to prune, the buds will be arranged along the stem at regular intervals in one of two ways: either alternately (one on one side of the stem, one farther up on the other side, and so on) or in opposite pairs (one on each side of the stem, directly opposite one another). The buds are usually closer together at the base of the stem and slightly wider apart as you progress upward.

If a plant has an alternate arrangement of buds, look from the tip of the stem downward and you may notice that the buds run in a spiral pattern down the stem. Where the buds are arranged in opposite pairs, look from the tip of the stem downward and you may notice that the pairs of buds are arranged roughly at right angles to one another. These bud (and leaf and stem) arrangements are designed to give each leaf the maximum amount of space and light.

On plants with the buds arranged alternately, any pruning cut should be at an angle, about 1–2in (2.5–5cm) above a bud, with the bud itself near the uppermost point of the cut. This is important because the healing of any cut is greatly influenced by the proximity of these growth buds. Usually, cuts are made to an outward-pointing bud to encourage an open structure of stems and branches. On plants with buds arranged in opposite pairs, any pruning cut should be about 1–2in (2.5–5cm) above a pair of buds, but at a right angle; this will leave a flat cut across the top of the shoot, so that both buds are left undamaged.

TIMING

Pruning is often done in winter because it is convenient for the gardener rather than ideal for the plant. Pruning is a good way to keep warm in the garden when the weather is chilly and the ground is wet or frozen, making it impossible to dig or

Prune plants grown for attractive fruits in late winter—once the birds have eaten the fruits.

cultivate the soil. At times like this, we rely on other gardening tasks, such as pruning, to keep us busy until the soil conditions improve.

As a rule, most deciduous plants are best pruned either after they have finished flowering or in the fall, winter, and early spring when they are dormant. However, as with most rules, there are exceptions for practical reasons. Plants that are grown for their attractive fruit will be left unpruned for several years to get a good display of hips or berries. Some plants don't respond well to pruning when they are dormant, especially in late winter or early spring, and pruning at the wrong time can kill a large section of the plant or, in extreme cases, the whole plant. For this reason some plants, such as birch (*Betula* spp.), buckeye or horse chestnut (*Aesculus* spp.), maple (*Acer* spp.), poplar (*Populus* spp.), and walnut (*Juglans* spp.), are pruned

PRUNING PLANTS WITH ALTERNATE BUDS
Make a sloping cut angled up toward the bud.

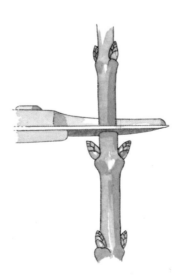

PRUNING PLANTS WITH OPPOSITE BUDS
Make a flat cut at right angles to the stem, just above a pair of buds.

in summer, when they are in full leaf, to protect them from bleeding copious quantities of sap. The leaves draw sap past the pruning wounds, keeping them relatively dry and reducing the chance of stems dying back.

Some plants are pruned at a particular time of year to protect them from specific pests or diseases. If fungal and bacterial plant diseases are common in your area, you will need to schedule pruning when the weather is dry. Dogwood anthrancnose and fire blight on crab apples (*Malus* spp.) can spread easily during wet spring weather.

AVOIDING DAMAGE

Pruning a plant creates wounds. Some will be quite small, but sometimes, as when branches are removed from a tree, they may be quite large. How quickly the wound heals over is a good measure of how healthy the plant is. However, it is a fact that pruning wounds, like any other injuries a plant might receive, are potential entry points for fungal or bacterial spores. Although the risk of diseases taking hold can never be wholly eliminated, you can reduce the risk by using sharp cutting tools to make clean, well-placed cuts.

For thousands of years, gardeners "helped" plants recover by smothering the wounds with paints and preparations to protect them. However, research has shown that covering a wound can actually seal in disease spores and encourage fungal rot.

Woody plants naturally produce chemical and physical barriers that resist the invasion of rot-causing organisms. The correct positioning of a clean cut offers more protection than any wound covering. On many plants, the natural barrier point is visible—it is the slightly swollen area where the lateral shoot or branch joins the main stem or trunk—and pruning at precisely this point improves the chances of the pruning wound healing quickly. For the same reason, any pruning cut on a branch should be about 1in (2.5cm) above a bud, because buds can produce chemicals that encourage wounds to heal quickly.

The only reason for painting over pruning cuts is purely cosmetic to cover a large, pale wound that contrasts with the darker color of the surrounding bark.

Prevent disease in Japanese maples by pruning in summer while they are actively growing. This will reduce the chance of fungal spores entering the open cuts.

PRUNING AND TRAINING

With many pruning techniques, making a good clean cut at the correct place on the plant is only part of the story. Often pruning is carried out in conjunction with some form of training, which can take the form of tying growths into a particular position, or trimming away shoots that are trying to grow in a certain direction. The use of canes or stakes to guide a plant's stems or shoots to grow in an upright position or the use of wires, trellis, and frames to steer growths in an angled or horizontal direction is usually practiced as the pruning is carried out.

It is important to remember that pruning cannot be carried out in isolation of other cultural practices when you are growing plants. Don't neglect your plants' nutritional needs, because removing large areas of leaf from growing plants (especially with summer pruning) can have a debilitating effect on them. Feeding, watering, and mulching are essential to maintain balanced, healthy growth and to help the plants to respond quickly after pruning is complete.

PINCHING

One of the main techniques you can use to shape a young plant is pinching. This involves removing the plant's growing point to encourage the sideshoots to develop. Since young shoots are often soft and sappy, you can snap off this growth with your thumb and pointer finger.

DEADHEADING

Plants flower to produce seeds. Once a flower is pollinated, it will gradually develop fruits with seeds inside, while an unpollinated flower will linger on the plant for much longer. As soon as seed is set, the plant will gradually produce fewer flowers and the garden display will look less impressive. So removing fading flowers from a plant will stimulate the rapid development of another flush of flowers, as happens with repeat-flowering roses.

This aspect of pruning is less important with plants such as species roses that flower only once, but deadheading may still keep the plant tidy and improve its appearance. For many plants, the best approach to deadheading the flowers is to remove only the flower and a short section of its supporting flower stalk, leaving as many leaves and sections of soft young stem as possible. These parts of the plant can still manufacture food to support the rest of the plant while it is growing.

Fan-training against a wall is an excellent way to grow larger plants in a confined space. It is important to allow younger, more productive shoots to replace older branches when you prune.

Deadhead on a regular basis to prevent the spent flowers from producing seeds. Deadheading will prolong the flowering period by encouraging a later flush of flowers.

DIRECTORY
OF PLANTS

This plant-by-plant guide, organized by botanical name, describes the best pruning methods for over 50 of the most widely grown garden plants. Explanations of formative, routine, and remedial pruning techniques are provided along with diagrams and detailed illustrations that show you exactly when and how to prune, and which tools to use.

ABELIA
Abelia

Glossy, dark green leaves and pretty flowers make abelias attractive additions to a mixed border or a sheltered wall or fence.

WHY PRUNE?

To encourage annual production and development of new shoots and to remove old, nonflowering wood.

PRUNING TIPS

Don't prune late-flowering plants immediately after flowering or the resultant new growth will be severely damaged by winter frosts.

WHEN TO PRUNE MOST SPECIES

Early or late spring

PLANTS PRUNED THIS WAY

- *Abelia floribunda*: in late spring and summer, after flowering
- *Abelia chinensis*: in early spring
- *Abelia ×grandiflora* and cvs.: in early spring
- *Abelia schumannii*: in early spring

WHICH TOOLS

- Hand pruners
- Long-handled pruners (loppers)
- Small pruning saw

FORMATIVE PRUNING

Prune young plants to encourage them to develop a bushy habit with strong shoots emerging from ground level. After planting, cut out any weak or damaged growth. Cut the remaining shoots back to about one-third of their length. This will encourage new shoots to develop from the plant's base as it becomes established.

ROUTINE PRUNING

Abelias usually produce new shoots from the base or low down on existing stems. Regular annual pruning to remove some of the oldest stems will give these new shoots room to grow. After flowering, cut out about one-quarter of the existing stems (choose the ones that look the oldest). Either cut them back to a healthy pair of buds or down to ground level. Remove any thin, weak shoots to avoid overcrowding. Cut out any frost-damaged shoots in late spring.

REMEDIAL PRUNING

If abelias are left unpruned for several years, they will produce large numbers of weak, short, thin stems and much poorer flowers, in terms of both size and quantity. In spring, cut all the stems back to within 6–8in (15–20cm) of ground level. In summer, remove up to one-third of the weakest and thinnest shoots to prevent overcrowding.

GENERAL HABIT OF
MATURE PLANT

Remove
thin, weak
shoots.

Cut back
to a healthy
pair of buds.

▬ Routine pruning
═ Dead and defective growth

ACTINIDIA
Chinese tara vine

This is a perfect climber for a sunny south- or southeast-facing wall close to a door or window— it will let you catch the full benefit of the delicately fragrant flowers in early summer.

WHY PRUNE?
To produce balanced growth and to control vigor.

PRUNING TIPS
Prune before growth starts.

WHEN TO PRUNE MOST SPECIES
Late winter or early spring

PLANTS PRUNED THIS WAY
- *Actinidia arguta* and cvs.: in late winter or early spring
- *Actinidia deliciosa (chinensis)* and cvs.: in late winter or early spring
- *Actinidia kolomikta* and cvs.: in late winter or early spring
- *Actinidia polygama* and cvs.: in late winter or early spring
- *Vitis* spp. and cvs.: in late winter or when plants are in full leaf

WHICH TOOLS
- Hand pruners
- Long-handled pruners (loppers)

FORMATIVE PRUNING
Prune young plants to encourage them to develop a framework of strong shoots emerging from the base. In the first spring after planting, cut out any weak or damaged growth. Cut all remaining stems back to a strong, healthy bud about 12in (30cm) above ground level. As the new shoots develop, select about six of the strongest ones for training onto the supporting structure. In the second spring, cut all sideshoots back by two-thirds, cut back any thin shoots to one or two buds, and remove any weak shoots altogether.

ROUTINE PRUNING
Try to produce a framework of strong, healthy shoots and encourage the formation of more healthy shoots. Also, prune mature plants to keep them contained within their allotted space. In late winter or early spring, shorten the main growths by cutting them back to about one-third or one-half of their original length. Tie them to a supporting framework. To prevent overcrowding, cut out any unneeded shoots. In summer, remove any overcrowded or crossing shoots. Cut out any old, bare stems close to ground level to make room for new growths.

REMEDIAL PRUNING
As they age, actinidias often become a tangled mass of old and new growth, and the overcrowding often leads to masses of poor, weak stems. They will, however, respond to hard pruning. In spring, cut the plant back to a framework of three or four main stems, each about 3ft (1m) long. Six to eight weeks after cutting back the plant, remove all weak, thin shoots, leaving up to six of the strongest, healthiest shoots to form a new framework. Train these into position.

GENERAL HABIT OF
MATURE PLANT

Tie in
main
growth.

FORMATIVE PRUNING

First spring

Remove
overcrowded or
crossing shoots.

■ Routine pruning
■ Dead and defective growth

AMELANCHIER
Juneberry, shadbush

There can be few more stunning sights than a mature amelanchier in full flower in midspring, when it foams with white blooms that emerge just as the leaves are beginning to unfurl.

WHY PRUNE?
To produce new growth and to improve flowering.

PRUNING TIPS
Always prune lightly to avoid overproduction of suckers.

WHEN TO PRUNE MOST SPECIES
Late spring

PLANTS PRUNED THIS WAY
- *Amelanchier asiatica*: in late spring, after flowering
- *Amelanchier arborea*: in late spring, after flowering
- *Amelanchier canadensis*: in late spring, after flowering
- *Amelanchier laevis*: in late spring, after flowering
- *Amelanchier lamarckii*: in late spring, after flowering

WHICH TOOLS
- Hand pruners
- Long-handled pruners (loppers)
- Pruning saw

FORMATIVE PRUNING
Prune young plants to encourage them to grow bushy, with strong shoots emerging from soil level. After planting, cut out any damaged growth. Cut the weaker shoots back to one or two buds above ground level to encourage new shoots to develop from the base of the plant as it becomes established.

ROUTINE PRUNING
These plants are usually grown as large, multistemmed shrubs. They generally produce new shoots from the base or low down on existing stems. Removing any overcrowded stems will encourage new shoots to form and give them space to grow. After flowering, thin out any congested or rubbing stems (choose the ones that look the oldest). Cut them back either to a healthy bud or to ground level. Remove any thin, weak shoots to avoid overcrowding. Alternatively, some species can be trained as trees. In this case, it is important to remove suckers growing around the trunk.

REMEDIAL PRUNING
If these plants are left unpruned for a number of years, they will produce large numbers of weak, thin stems, creating a thicket of overcrowded stems that can twist around one another. In spring, cut all stems back to within 3–10in (7–25cm) of ground level. In summer, remove up to one-third of the weakest and thinnest shoots to prevent overcrowding.

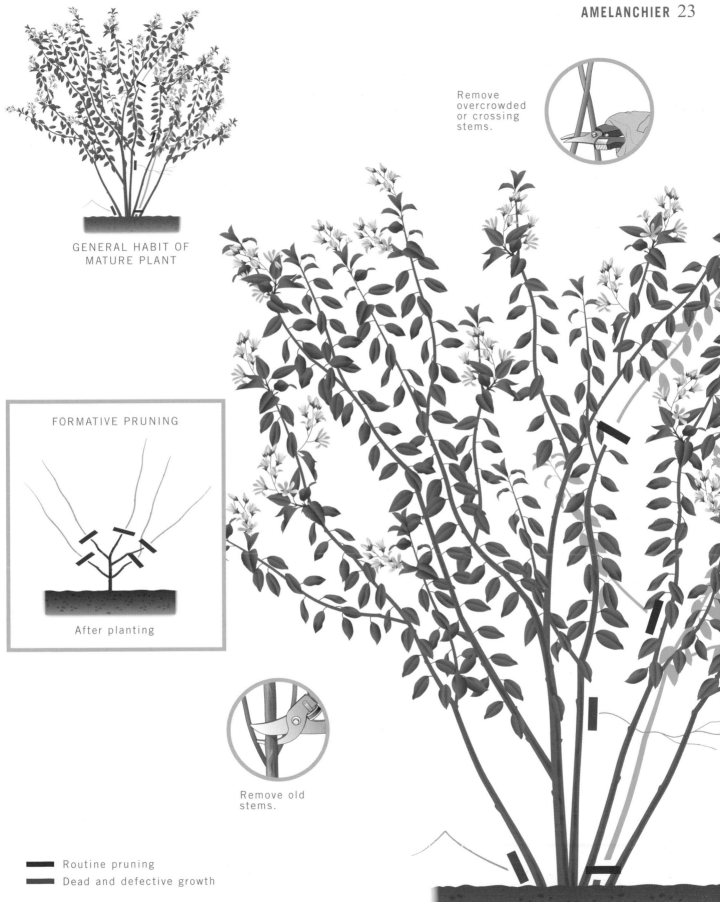

GENERAL HABIT OF
MATURE PLANT

Remove
overcrowded
or crossing
stems.

FORMATIVE PRUNING

After planting

Remove old
stems.

■ Routine pruning
■ Dead and defective growth

AUCUBA JAPONICA
Spotted laurel

Guaranteed to brighten a shady corner where little else will grow, spotted laurel has handsome, glossy leaves and a neat, rounded shape.

WHY PRUNE?

To keep a well-balanced and rounded shape and to prevent the plants from becoming bare and straggly at the base.

PRUNING TIPS

Prune in spring after the risk of frost has passed to reduce the chances of late frosts damaging new growth.

WHEN TO PRUNE MOST SPECIES

Midspring

PLANTS PRUNED THIS WAY

- *Aucuba japonica* and cvs.: in midspring, after the berries have faded
- *Daphne odora* and cvs.: in late spring, after the flowers have faded
- *Enkianthus chinensis*: in midspring, after the flowers have faded
- *Skimmia japonica*: in midspring, after the berries have faded

WHICH TOOLS

- Hand pruners
- Long-handled pruners (loppers)

FORMATIVE PRUNING

Prune young plants to encourage them to develop a bushy habit with strong shoots emerging 6–8in (15–20cm) above ground level. After planting, cut out any weak or damaged growth. Cut the remaining shoots back by about one-third to encourage new shoots to develop from the base of the plant as it becomes established.

ROUTINE PRUNING

Prune lightly in spring after the brightly colored berries have finished their display and after the risk of severe frost has passed. Try to maintain a well-balanced overall shape with healthy, glossy foliage. Cut any excessively vigorous shoots back to help the plant retain its natural shape. Remove any all-green shoots that have developed on variegated plants to prevent them from reverting back to the all-green characteristics of the parent plants. Prune back to healthy growth any shoots that show signs of frost damage or dieback.

REMEDIAL PRUNING

Aucubas have a natural tendency to produce long, bare shoots with only a few leaves on the ends, and they often become bare at the base, revealing dull green stems. In the first year, remove half of the main shoots to within 6–8in (15–20cm) of ground level. Cut down to ground level any thin, weak shoots. In the second year, cut the remaining old stems down to 6–8in (15–20cm) above ground level. Remove any thin, spindly growth that developed as a result of the previous year's pruning.

GENERAL HABIT OF
MATURE PLANT

Remove dead or
damaged stems.

Remove
overvigorous
stems.

Routine pruning
Dead and defective growth

BERBERIS
(deciduous species)
Berberis, barberry

Berberis are good-value shrubs, providing leaf color, flowers, and berries, even in unpromising conditions.

WHY PRUNE?

To make sure that a supply of new shoots emerges from ground level each year.

PRUNING TIPS

Wait until summer to remove dead wood—it is much easier to see then.

WHEN TO PRUNE MOST SPECIES

Early summer

PLANTS PRUNED THIS WAY

- *Berberis ×ottawensis*: in early summer, immediately after flowering
- *Berberis ×rubrostilla*: in early summer, immediately after flowering
- *Berberis thunbergii*: in early summer, immediately after flowering
- *Berberis wilsoniae*: in early summer, immediately after flowering

WHICH TOOLS

- Hand pruners
- Long-handled pruners (loppers)
- Thornproof leather gloves

FORMATIVE PRUNING

Prune young plants to encourage them to develop a bushy habit with strong shoots emerging from ground level. After planting, cut out any weak or damaged growth. Lightly pinch back the remaining shoots to about two-thirds of their length so that the plant will form new shoots from the base.

ROUTINE PRUNING

If they are to flower well, berberis need regular annual pruning to remove a proportion of the old wood and to encourage new flower-bearing shoots. Also, if you have a plant with purple or variegated leaves you should prune so that young shoots, which tend to have more attractive color, replace old ones. Immediately after flowering in early summer, cut the old flower-bearing stems back to a strong pair of buds or to lower, younger shoots. This will eliminate the fruits, which can be spread easily by birds, and will give the maximum period of growth to produce a good display of flowers the following year. On mature shrubs try to remove between one-quarter and one-fifth of the old stems each year to allow light in and to make room for new shoots.

REMEDIAL PRUNING

Berberis tend to form a matted clump of branches, and the inner branches often shed their leaves and die from lack of light. Plants respond well to severe pruning. In early summer, remove all dead or weak shoots. Cut all healthy stems back to within 12in (30cm) of ground level.

Cut back
to a healthy
pair of buds.

GENERAL HABIT OF
MATURE PLANT

Remedial pruning: Cut
out old stems just above
a replacement shoot.

Remove
old
stems.

━━━ Routine pruning
━━━ Dead and defective growth

BERBERIS
(evergreen species)
Berberis, barberry

These useful shrubs provide year-round foliage
as well as good flower and berry color.

FORMATIVE PRUNING

Prune young plants to encourage them to develop a bushy habit
with strong shoots emerging from ground level. After planting,
cut out any weak or damaged growth. Leave the plant to become
established for one year. In its second year, remove all the old
shoots, leaving only the young, vigorous growth that developed
in the first year.

ROUTINE PRUNING

These plants need regular annual pruning to replace the old stems,
which would gradually accumulate and clog up the center of the
shrub, and to encourage new flower-bearing shoots. Immediately
after flowering or in early summer, cut the old flower-bearing
stems back to a strong pair of buds or cut down to lower, younger
shoots. This will sacrifice the berries but will give the maximum
period of growth for a good display of flowers the following year.
On mature shrubs, try to remove from one-quarter to one-fifth of
the old stems each year to allow light in and make room for new
shoots to develop.

REMEDIAL PRUNING

Berberis tend to form a matted clump of branches, and the inner
branches often shed their leaves and die from lack of light. In
these circumstances, the only growth that occurs is around the
edges of the plant. Plants respond well to severe pruning. In early
summer, remove all dead or weak shoots. Cut all healthy stems
back to within 12in (30cm) of ground level.

GENERAL HABIT OF
MATURE PLANT

Cut back
to a healthy
pair of buds.

Remove
old stems.

▬ Routine pruning
▬ Dead and defective growth

BOUGAINVILLEA

Bougainvillea, paper flower

The vividly colored flowers, so prolifically borne that they almost obscure the foliage, are a spectacular sight from summer into fall.

WHY PRUNE?
To encourage new shoots to replace the old ones and to promote regular flowering.

PRUNING TIPS
Handle the stems by gripping them at the top, because the thorns are angled down the stem.

WHEN TO PRUNE MOST SPECIES
Early spring

PLANTS PRUNED THIS WAY
- *Bougainvillea* ×*buttiana* and cvs.: in early spring, after the bracts have faded
- *Bougainvillea glabra* and cvs.: in early spring, after the bracts have faded
- *Bougainvillea spectabilis* and cvs.: in late summer, after the bracts have faded

WHICH TOOLS
- Hand pruners
- Long-handled pruners (loppers)
- Thornproof leather gloves

FORMATIVE PRUNING
Prune young plants to encourage a framework of strong shoots emerging from the base of the plant. In the first spring after planting, cut out any weak or damaged growth. Then cut all strong, healthy stems back to 12in (30cm) above ground level. As new shoots develop, tie the strongest ones onto the supporting structure.

ROUTINE PRUNING
Try to produce a framework of strong, healthy shoots to encourage the formation of flower-producing spurs. Also, prune mature plants to contain them within their allotted area. Reduce the length of the main growths by cutting them back to about two-thirds of their original length and tie them into place on the supporting structure. To prevent overcrowding, cut out any unneeded shoots. Cut all lateral shoots back to within two or three buds of the main stems—these will bear the current season's flowers and bracts.

REMEDIAL PRUNING
Unless they are pruned regularly, bougainvilleas grow into a tangled mass of old and new growth, and the overcrowding often leads to pests and diseases. In spring, use pruners or, if the branches and shoots are very thick, long-handled pruners (loppers) to cut the plant back to a framework of three or four main branches, each about 3ft (1m) long. This will encourage new shoots. Six to eight weeks after cutting back the branches, remove all weak, thin shoots. Leaving up to about six of the strongest, healthiest shoots to produce flowers, remove three or four of the oldest stems and train replacements into position.

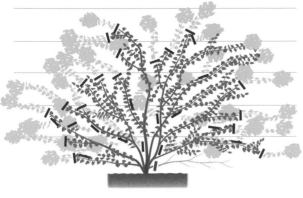

GENERAL HABIT OF
MATURE PLANT

Remove
overcrowded
stems.

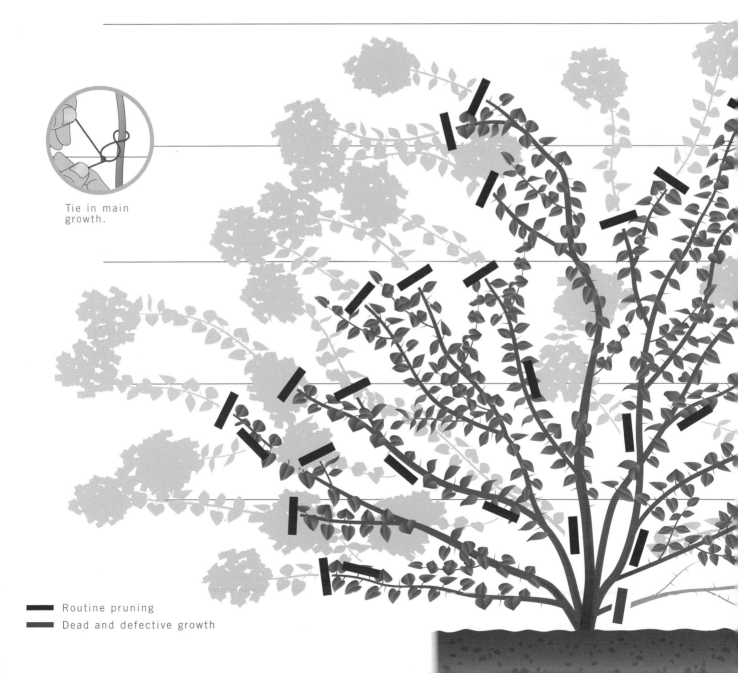

Tie in main
growth.

■ Routine pruning
■ Dead and defective growth

BUDDLEJA DAVIDII

Buddleia, butterfly bush

This tough, reliable, and showy shrub is always popular with new gardeners, simply because few plants are easier to grow.

WHY PRUNE?
To encourage strong growth and the production of larger, more attractive flower spikes.

PRUNING TIPS
Use bypass pruners because anvil-type pruners may crush the stems.

WHEN TO PRUNE MOST SPECIES
Early or midspring

PLANTS PRUNED THIS WAY
- *Buddleja crispa* and cvs.: in midspring, after the risk of frost has passed
- *Buddleja fallowiana* and cvs.: in midspring, after the risk of frost has passed
- *Buddleja globosa* and cvs.: in late winter, before fresh growth appears

WHICH TOOLS
- Hand pruners
- Long-handled pruners (loppers)
- Pruning saw

FORMATIVE PRUNING

Young plants should be pruned to encourage a bushy shape with strong shoots emerging from about 12in (30cm) above soil level. In spring, just as the new growth starts, cut out any thin, weak growth or damaged shoots. Cut back the remaining stems to three or four pairs of buds to develop a framework of new shoots from 12in (30cm) above the base of the plant so that a short trunk or leg forms as it becomes established.

ROUTINE PRUNING

Buddleia needs regular annual pruning to remove the old flowering wood, which would accumulate and cause overcrowding, and to encourage the production of new, flower-bearing shoots. In spring, cut back all the old flower-bearing stems to two or three pairs of buds or shoots to allow the maximum period of growth for a good display of flowers in summer and fall. Cut back into older growth if a branch or stem has to be removed completely or, if possible, cut just above a healthy pair of buds. Always cut back any thin, weak shoots to their point of origin because they are likely to succumb to pests and diseases and rarely produce good flowers.

REMEDIAL PRUNING

Left unpruned, buddleias develop into dense, overcrowded shrubs. They grow lots of thin, weak, arching stems that produce few flowers. This can be overcome with hard pruning, or cutting the plant down to its original stem or leg. In spring, depending on the thickness of the branches and shoots, use a saw or long-handled pruners (loppers) to cut the plant back to its original framework, encouraging new growth to replace the old shoots. A month after the initial pruning, remove all the weak, thin, sappy young shoots and leave up to eight of the strongest, healthiest shoots to produce flowers and form a new framework for future years.

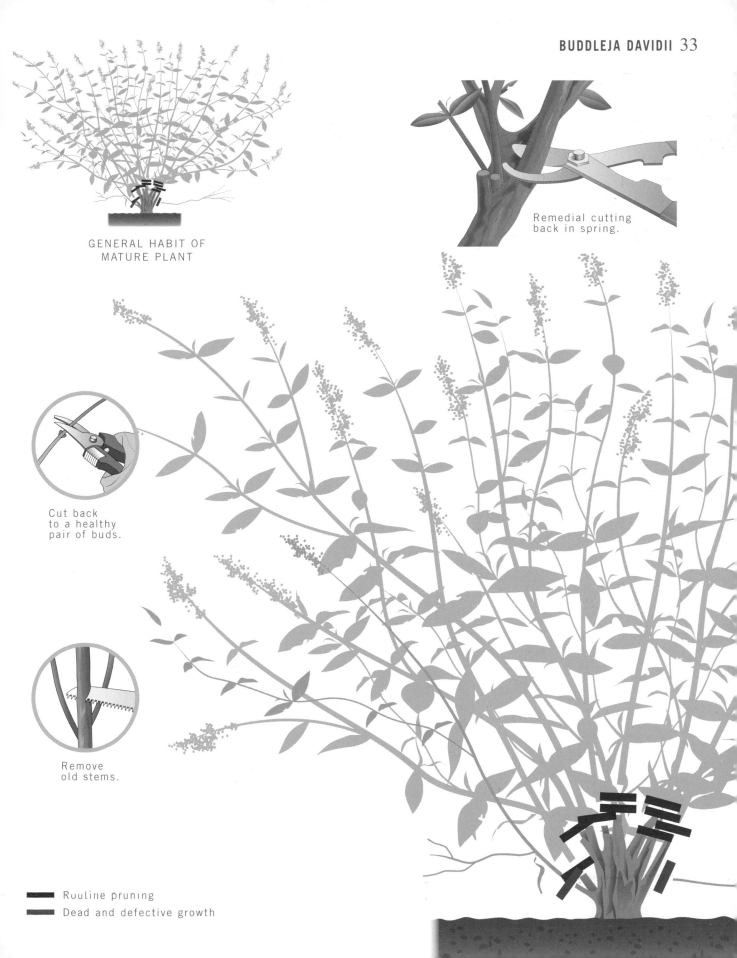

GENERAL HABIT OF
MATURE PLANT

Remedial cutting
back in spring.

Cut back
to a healthy
pair of buds.

Remove
old stems.

■ Routine pruning
■ Dead and defective growth

CALLICARPA
Callicarpa, beautyberry

Callicarpas are grown for their small, round, brightly colored fruits, which are borne in generous clusters after a long, hot summer and last well into the winter.

WHY PRUNE?
To replace the older stems with new ones and to remove frost-damaged shoots.

PRUNING TIPS
Cut frost-damaged stems down to ground level, and they will shoot again from the base.

WHEN TO PRUNE MOST SPECIES
Midspring

PLANTS PRUNED THIS WAY
- *Callicarpa bodinieri* and cvs.: in early spring
- *Callicarpa japonica* and cvs.: in midspring
- *Callicarpa rubella* and cvs.: in midspring

WHICH TOOLS
- Hand pruners
- Pruning saw

FORMATIVE PRUNING

Prune young plants to encourage them to develop a bushy habit with strong shoots emerging from just above ground level. In spring, just as the new growth starts, cut out any weak or damaged growth. Then cut the remaining shoots back to three or four buds above ground level.

ROUTINE PRUNING

If they are to flower well, callicarpas need regular annual pruning to remove the old wood and to encourage new flower-bearing shoots. In midspring after the risk of frost has passed, cut the oldest shoots down to ground level. Aim to take out between one-fifth and one-quarter of the growth each year, always selecting the oldest wood or any damaged or broken shoots for pruning. Cut the previous year's flower-bearing stems back by at least half, pruning just above a healthy bud or a well-placed new sideshoot.

REMEDIAL PRUNING

These shrubs will naturally become thick and overcrowded as they age, producing fewer flowers and fruits and becoming increasingly susceptible to pests and diseases, especially if the pruning has been neglected. In spring, leave just three or four strong stems and cut the remaining shoots back to within 2–3in (5–7cm) of ground level to encourage new shoots that will replace the old ones. The following year, completely remove any thin or weak shoots. Cut out the three or four remaining old stems close to ground level.

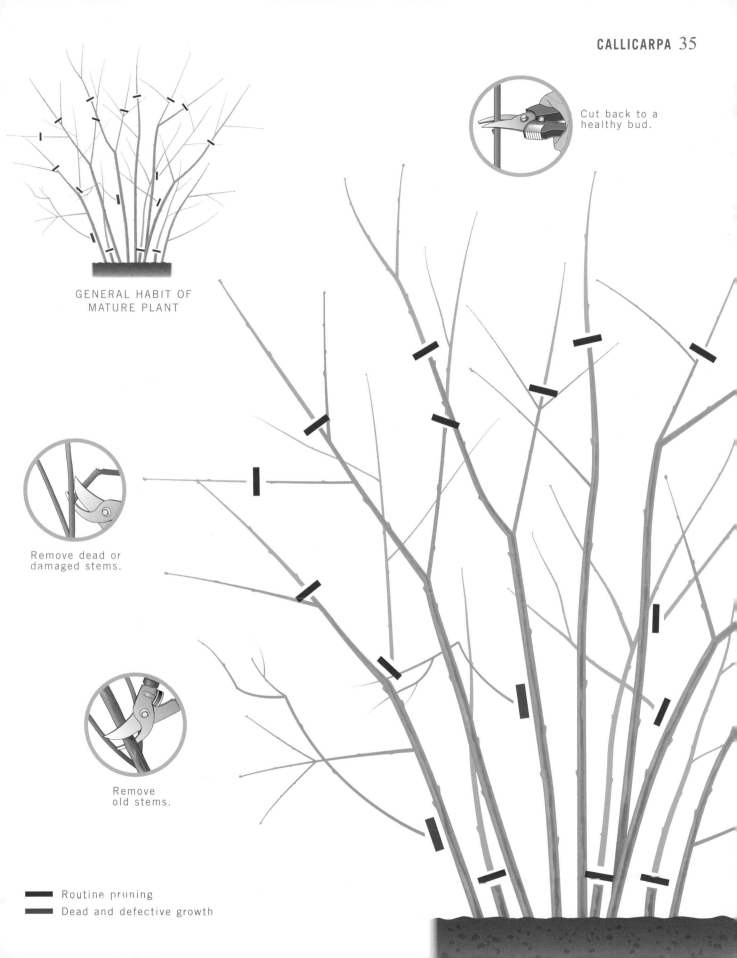

GENERAL HABIT OF
MATURE PLANT

Cut back to a
healthy bud.

Remove dead or
damaged stems.

Remove
old stems.

Routine pruning
Dead and defective growth

CALLISTEMON
Bottlebrush

Callistemons are grown for their fantastic displays of bristlelike blooms. They often make the plant look as if it has caught fire, especially when the branches are swaying in the wind.

WHY PRUNE?
To prevent the plant from becoming straggly and untidy.

PRUNING TIPS
Cut back to strong, healthy buds.

WHEN TO PRUNE MOST SPECIES
Late summer

PLANTS PRUNED THIS WAY
- *Callistemon citrinus* and cvs.: in late summer, after flowering
- *Callistemon rigidus*: in late summer, after flowering

WHICH TOOLS
- Hand pruners
- Long-handled pruners (loppers)

FORMATIVE PRUNING

Prune young plants to encourage them to grow bushy, with strong shoots emerging from low down on the stems. After planting, cut out any weak or damaged growth. Lightly pinch back the remaining shoots to about two-thirds of their length to encourage new shoots to develop from the base of the plant as it becomes established.

ROUTINE PRUNING

These plants do not need regular annual pruning to flower well. However, they are pruned to avoid long, straggly stems with lots of bare wood and to encourage the production of new flower-bearing shoots. Immediately after flowering, cut the old flower-bearing stems back to a healthy bud. This will allow the maximum period of growth to produce a good display of flowers the following year.

REMEDIAL PRUNING

Callistemons naturally produce long, straggly stems, and plants can look open and untidy, especially if the pruning has been neglected. This can be overcome with hard pruning, which must be done in stages over two or three years rather than just cutting the plant down completely. Each year, remove one or two stems after flowering, cutting them back to within 2–3in (5–7cm) of ground level to encourage new shoots to replace the old ones.

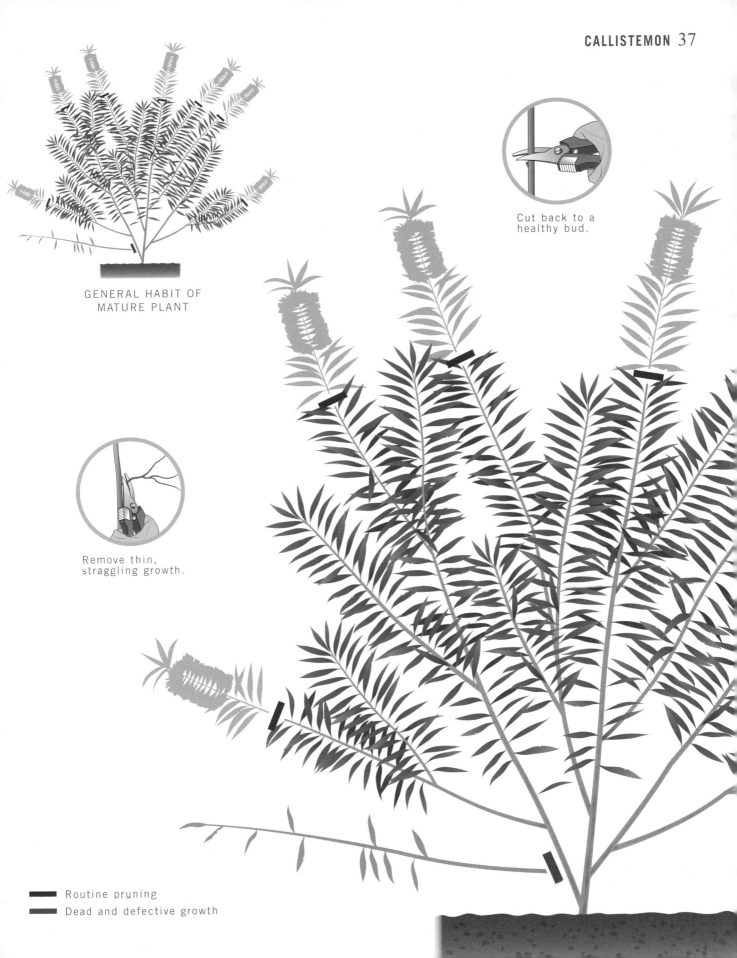

GENERAL HABIT OF
MATURE PLANT

Cut back to a
healthy bud.

Remove thin,
straggling growth.

Routine pruning
Dead and defective growth

CALLUNA
Heather, Scots heather, ling

Heathers are hardy, compact, evergreen shrubs available in a wide range of foliage and flower colors, providing interest in the garden all year round.

WHY PRUNE?
To promote new flower-bearing shoots and keep the plant tidy.

PRUNING TIPS
Calluna vulgaris can be pruned just after flowering in milder climates.

WHEN TO PRUNE MOST SPECIES
Late winter or early spring

PLANTS PRUNED THIS WAY
- *Calluna vulgaris*: in late winter or early spring, after flowering
- *Erica carnea* and cvs.: in midspring, after flowering but before new growth starts
- *Erica cinerea* and cvs.: in early spring, after flowering
- *Erica ×darleyensis* and cvs.: in midspring, after flowering but before new growth starts

WHICH TOOLS
- Hand pruners
- Pruning shears

FORMATIVE PRUNING
Prune young plants to encourage them to form a bushy shape with many shoots emerging from ground level. After planting, cut out any weak or damaged growth. Cut the remaining shoots back to one-third of their original length.

ROUTINE PRUNING
Try to prevent the plant from becoming too straggly and open in the center. In late winter or early spring, trim back all old flower-bearing shoots to just below the dead flowers. Use hand pruners to cut back any long, straggling growths to make them branch.

REMEDIAL PRUNING
These low-growing shrubs often become open and bare in the center. They do respond to severe pruning, but it is usually better to remove and replace old, straggly plants. Dig up and dispose of old, overgrown plants.

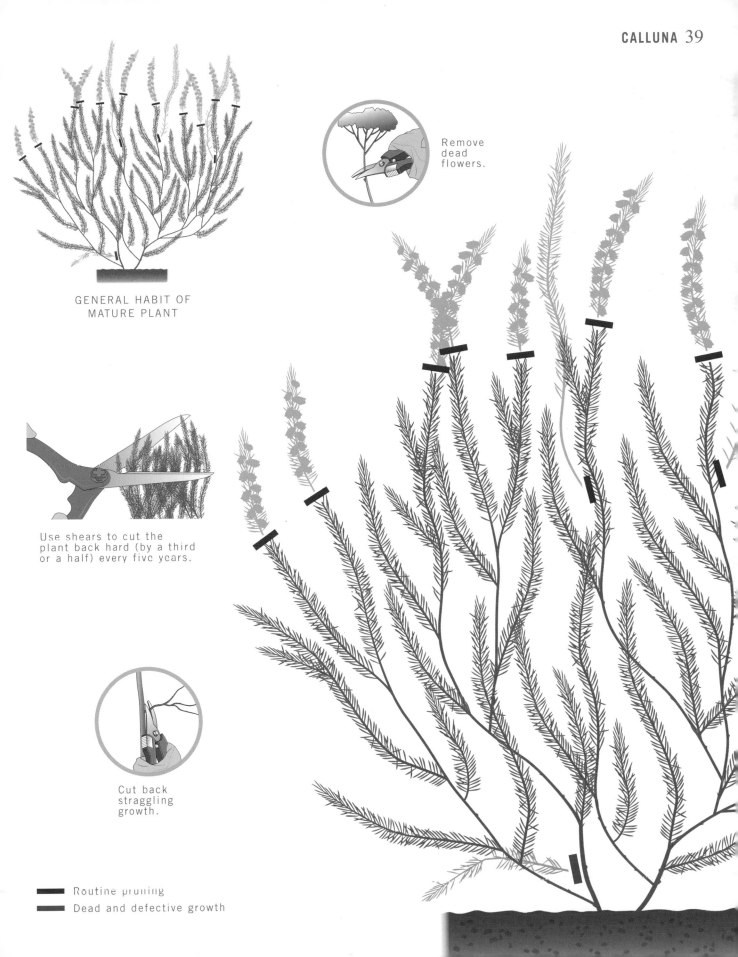

GENERAL HABIT OF
MATURE PLANT

Remove
dead
flowers.

Use shears to cut the
plant back hard (by a third
or a half) every five years.

Cut back
straggling
growth.

▬▬ Routine pruning
▬▬ Dead and defective growth

CAMELLIA
Camellia

In late winter and early spring, the beautiful flowers of camellias are a welcome promise that warmer weather is on the way.

WHY PRUNE?
To develop a healthy, bushy, free-flowering plant.

PRUNING TIPS
Prune soon after flowering, just before the plant begins its main growing period.

WHEN TO PRUNE MOST SPECIES
Midspring

PLANTS PRUNED THIS WAY
- *Camellia japonica* and cvs.: in spring, after flowering
- *Camellia reticulata* and cvs.: in spring, after flowering
- *Camellia sasanqua* and cvs.: in spring, before new growth starts
- *Camellia ×williamsii* and cvs.: in spring, after flowering

WHICH TOOLS
- Hand pruners
- Long-handled pruners (loppers)
- Pruning saw

FORMATIVE PRUNING
Prune young plants to create a bushy, well-structured shrub with plenty of branches growing close to ground level. In spring, cut any weak, leggy shoots back to about two or three buds. Remove the top one-third of any long, straggling shoots.

ROUTINE PRUNING
Camellias grow quite happily for many years with little or no pruning. However, if you shorten the previous season's growth by cutting close to the old wood immediately after flowering, you are more likely to have a bushy, free-flowering plant. This is also a good way to keep the plant from getting too bare and leggy. In spring, immediately after the flowers have fallen, cut the flower-bearing shoots back to within three to five buds of the old wood. This will encourage the plant to develop many short, flowering stems for the following year. In summer, shorten by one-third any overly vigorous shoots to prevent the plant from becoming unbalanced and lopsided.

REMEDIAL PRUNING
In time, camellias often become bare and leggy at the base. They respond well to remedial pruning, but this should be phased over two years. Do not cut the plant back in one operation. In spring after flowering, cut the thickest branches down to 2ft (60cm) above ground level. The following year, cut any remaining old branches down to the same height. If necessary, thin some of the new shoots to prevent overcrowding.

GENERAL HABIT OF
MATURE PLANT

After flowering,
cut back old
flower-bearing
stems.

Shorten
overvigorous
stems.

Routine pruning
Dead and defective growth

CEANOTHUS
(deciduous species)
Ceanothus, California lilac

Blue ceanothus is a wonderful sight in a summer garden, as are the rarer pink-flowered species, which flower as abundantly.

WHY PRUNE?

To keep the plant growing well and producing new growth and flowers.

PRUNING TIPS

Use sharp tools that will cut cleanly through the stems, because crushed or bruised tissue tends to die back.

WHEN TO PRUNE MOST SPECIES

Early or midspring

PLANTS PRUNED THIS WAY

- *Ceanothus* 'Gloire de Versailles': in early spring, before new growth starts
- *Ceanothus* ×*delileanus* and cvs.: in midspring, before new growth starts
- *Ceanothus* ×*pallidus* and cvs.: in midspring, before new growth starts

WHICH TOOLS

- Hand pruners
- Long-handled pruners (loppers)
- Pruning saw

FORMATIVE PRUNING

Prune young plants to encourage them to develop a bushy habit with strong shoots emerging from just above ground level. In the first spring after planting, cut out any weak or damaged growth. Then cut all strong, healthy stems back to about one-third of their original length. The following spring, cut all the main stems back to one-third of their original length. Shorten all sideshoots to within 6in (15cm) of the main stems.

ROUTINE PRUNING

Established plants often become large, open, and rather straggly. To avoid this, prune them annually when they reach 3–4ft (1–1.2m) high. In addition, remove any weak shoots, which can cause overcrowding. In spring before new growth starts, cut all shoots back to within three or four buds of the previous season's growth. Remove any dead stems from the center of the plant.

REMEDIAL PRUNING

Left unpruned, ceanothus will develop into open, sprawling shrubs, often with splitting and breaking branches. Hard pruning can overcome this, as can cutting the plant down to its original stem about 12in (30cm) above ground level. In spring, cut the plant back to its original framework to encourage new shoots to develop. Depending on the thickness of the branches and shoots, use a pruning saw or long-handled pruners (loppers).

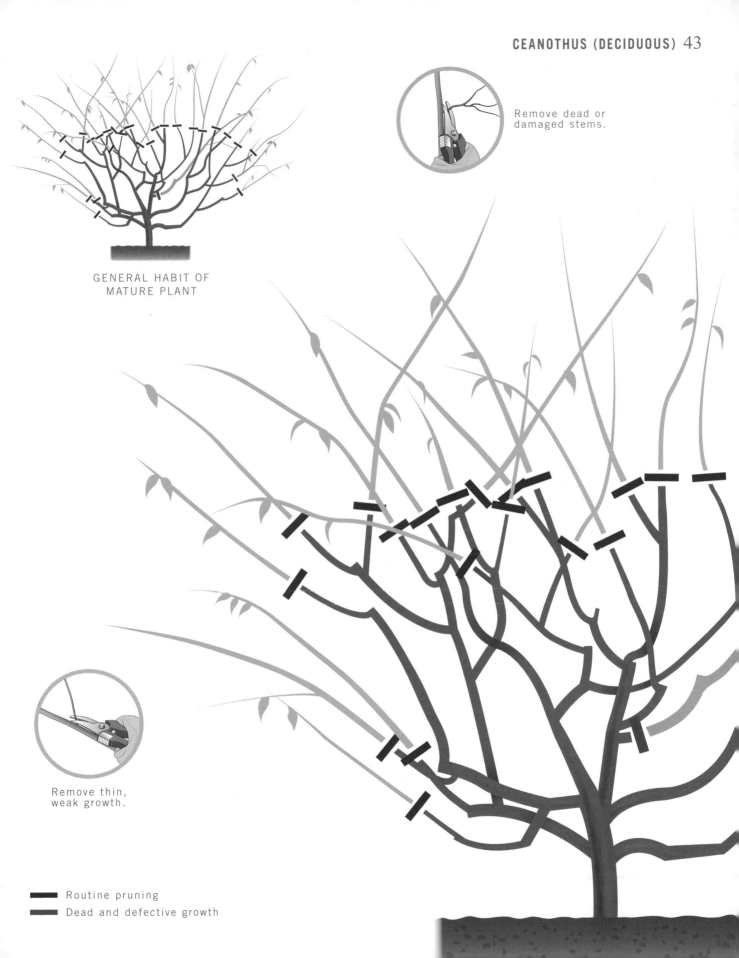

Remove dead or damaged stems.

GENERAL HABIT OF
MATURE PLANT

Remove thin,
weak growth.

■ Routine pruning
■ Dead and defective growth

CEANOTHUS
(evergreen species)
Ceanothus, California lilac

Few shrubs bear blue flowers, and evergreen ceanothus are doubly valued—for their year-round foliage and for their beautiful blooms.

WHY PRUNE?
To keep the plant growing well and producing new growth and flowers.

PRUNING TIPS
Don't prune back into old, bare wood, because it rarely produces new shoots.

WHEN TO PRUNE MOST SPECIES
Early spring or midsummer

PLANTS PRUNED THIS WAY
- *Ceanothus arboreus* and cvs.: in midsummer, after flowering
- *Ceanothus impressus* and cvs.: in midsummer, after flowering
- *Ceanothus thyrsiflorus* and cvs.: in midsummer, after flowering
- *Ceanothus* 'Burkwoodii': in early spring, before new growth starts

WHICH TOOLS
- Hand pruners
- Long-handled pruners (loppers)
- Pruning saw

FORMATIVE PRUNING
Prune young plants to encourage them to develop a bushy habit with strong shoots emerging from just above ground level. In the first spring after planting, cut out any weak or damaged growth. Pinch off the tips of the main shoots by removing about one-third of each shoot.

ROUTINE PRUNING
To prevent the plants from becoming too dense and overcrowded and to keep them flowering regularly, you need to prune them regularly. If they become too large, they often fall over because of root damage. Plants that flower in spring or early summer should be pruned in midsummer; cut all flower-bearing shoots back by removing one-third from the ends. Plants that flower in midsummer and fall are pruned in spring; cut all flower-bearing shoots back by removing the end third.

REMEDIAL PRUNING
Evergreen ceanothus sometimes become bare at the base. They do not respond well to severe pruning, however, so it is easier to replace old plants than to revive them. Dig up the old plant and replace it. Completely replace the soil in the planting hole when you do so.

GENERAL HABIT OF
MATURE PLANT

Cut back
overvigorous
stems.

Remove old
flower-bearing
stems.

▬ Routine pruning
▬ Dead and defective growth

CERCIS
Redbud

These remarkable trees or shrubs produce small, pealike flowers on bare branches (even on the main trunk) before the leaves emerge in spring. Before they drop in fall, the leaves turn a pretty buttery yellow.

WHY PRUNE?
To remove damaged or overcrowded growth and to develop a strong structure.

PRUNING TIPS
Wait until the new growth starts before pruning.

WHEN TO PRUNE MOST SPECIES
Early summer

PLANTS PRUNED THIS WAY
- *Cercis canadensis* and cvs.: in early summer, after flowering
- *Cercis siliquastrum* and cvs.: in early summer, after flowering

WHICH TOOLS
- Hand pruners
- Long-handled pruners (loppers)
- Pruning saw

FORMATIVE PRUNING
Prune young plants to encourage them to grow bushy, with strong shoots emerging 2–3ft (60cm–1m) above soil level. After planting, cut out any damaged growth. Cut the main stem back to about 3ft (1m) above ground level to encourage the development of new shoots that will create a multistemmed tree as it becomes established.

ROUTINE PRUNING
These plants are usually grown as small trees or multistemmed shrubs and are pruned to remove overcrowded or damaged stems, or to lift the canopy when drooping branches are a problem. After flowering, remove any broken, frost-damaged, or rubbing stems, cutting them back to a healthy bud. Remove any thin, weak shoots to avoid overcrowding.

REMEDIAL PRUNING
These plants often produce stems and branches with sharply angled crotches, which can split in strong, gusting winds. Plants will, however, respond well to severe pruning. In late spring or early summer, use a saw or long-handled pruners (loppers), depending on the thickness of the branches and shoots, to cut the plant back to a framework of branches 2–3ft (60cm–1m) above soil level. This will encourage new shoots to develop. Six to eight weeks after cutting down the plant, remove all the weak, thin shoots, leaving up to six of the strongest, healthiest shoots.

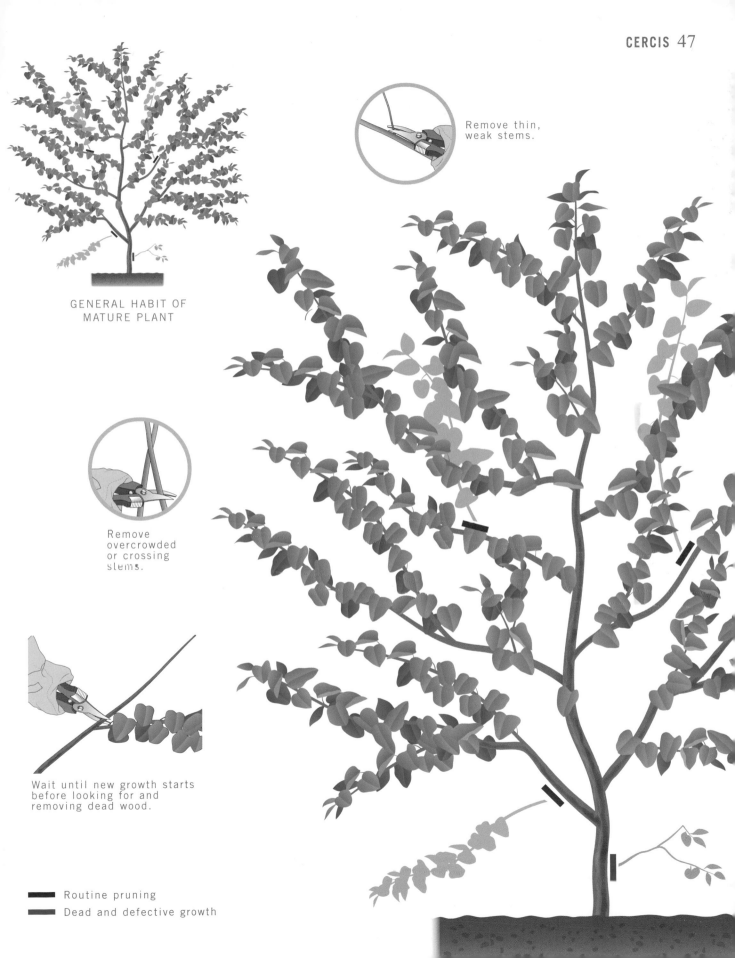

GENERAL HABIT OF
MATURE PLANT

Remove thin,
weak stems.

Remove
overcrowded
or crossing
stems.

Wait until new growth starts
before looking for and
removing dead wood.

▬ Routine pruning
▬ Dead and defective growth

CHAENOMELES
Flowering quince, Japanese quince

This is one of the most popular early-flowering shrubs and an excellent freestanding shrub, wall shrub, or flowering hedge.

WHY PRUNE?
To replace old growth with new flower-bearing shoots.

PRUNING TIPS
Prune plants in alternate years if you want a display of fruits.

WHEN TO PRUNE MOST SPECIES
Late spring or early summer

PLANTS PRUNED THIS WAY
- *Chaenomeles ×californica* and cvs.: after flowering
- *Chaenomeles cathayensis*: after flowering
- *Chaenomeles japonica* and cvs.: after flowering
- *Chaenomeles speciosa* and cvs.: after flowering
- *Chaenomeles ×superba* and cvs.: after flowering

WHICH TOOLS
- Hand pruners
- Long-handled pruners (loppers)
- Pruning saw
- Thornproof leather gloves

FORMATIVE PRUNING

Freestanding and wall-trained shrubs are grown as multistemmed plants, with strong shoots emerging from just above ground level. In the first spring after planting, as the new growth starts, cut out any thin, weak growth or damaged shoots. Cut the remaining shoots back to about two-thirds of their existing length.

ROUTINE PRUNING

Flowering quinces will grow quite well with little or no pruning, but they tend to become congested, which leads to smaller and fewer flowers and invites disease. Regular pruning will encourage the plant to replace old, nonproductive growth with new, flower-bearing shoots and will improve air circulation within the plant. After flowering, in late spring or early summer, remove any crossing or rubbing branches and thin out congested shoots. Cut out one or two of the very old stems each year to make room for replacement branches. Cut any sideshoots back to three or four leaves, which will form next year's flowering spurs. On wall-trained shrubs, tie the new growth to form a fan-shaped plant after pruning, leaving 6–8in (15–20cm) between stems.

REMEDIAL PRUNING

When plants are allowed to become congested, the inner branches will often shed their leaves and die from lack of light, so that the only growth is around the edges. These plants respond well to severe pruning, but it should be done in stages over two or three years. Cut about one-third of the stems back to within 6in (15cm) of ground level. Repeat this process over the next two or three years until the old growth has been removed and replaced.

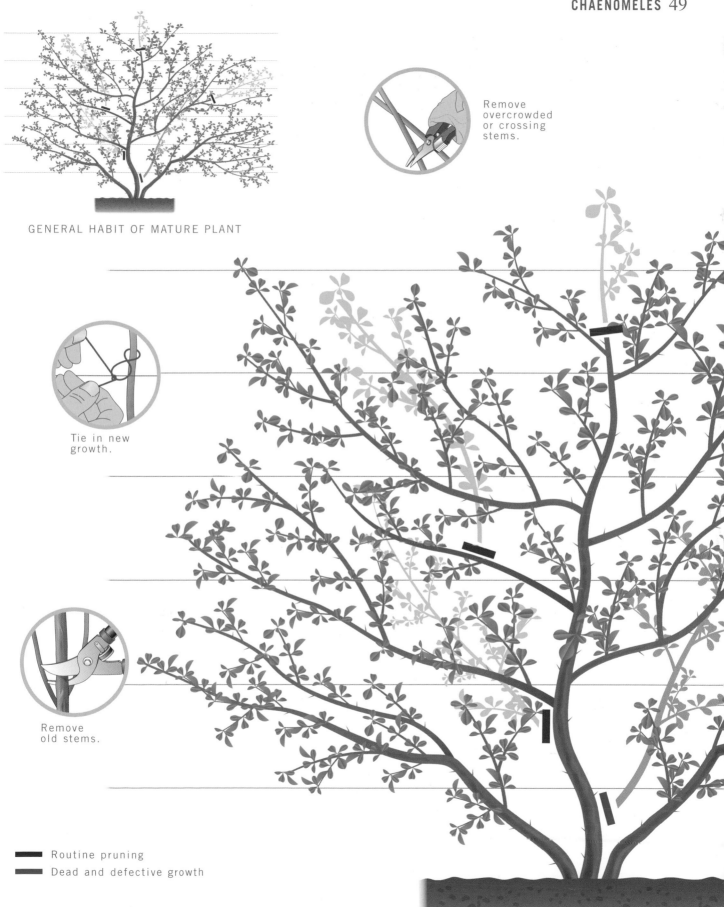

GENERAL HABIT OF MATURE PLANT

Remove overcrowded or crossing stems.

Tie in new growth.

Remove old stems.

Routine pruning

Dead and defective growth

CHOISYA
Mexican orange blossom

This popular evergreen shrub has aromatic leaves and bears fragrant flowers twice a year. Plant close to a path or house window to get maximum benefit from the flowers.

WHY PRUNE?
To keep the plant growing well and producing new growth and flowers.

PRUNING TIPS
Prune in late spring so that the new shoots are not unduly damaged by frost.

WHEN TO PRUNE MOST SPECIES
Late spring

PLANTS PRUNED THIS WAY
- *Choisya arizonica* and cvs.: in late spring; after flowering
- *Choisya ternata* and cvs.: in late spring, after flowering

WHICH TOOLS
- Hand pruners
- Long-handled pruners (loppers)

FORMATIVE PRUNING
Prune young plants to encourage them to grow bushy, with strong shoots emerging 6–8in (15–20cm) above soil level. After planting, cut out any weak or damaged growth, and cut the remaining shoots back by about one-third to encourage the development of new shoots from the base of the plant.

ROUTINE PRUNING
Prune in spring, immediately after flowering and after the risk of severe frost has passed. Try to encourage the plant to develop and maintain a well-balanced shape and encourage the production of a second flush of blooms. Prune back any excessively vigorous shoots to help the plant retain its natural shape. Cut the old flower-bearing stems back by 8–12in (20–30cm). Prune any shoots that show signs of frost damage or dieback.

REMEDIAL PRUNING
These shrubs often develop bare stems at the base and open, straggly growth. Fortunately, they respond well to remedial pruning. In spring, cut all of the main shoots back to within 6–8in (15–20cm) of soil level. Cut down to ground level any thin, weak shoots. During the second year, remove any thin, spindly growths that have developed as a result of the previous year's pruning.

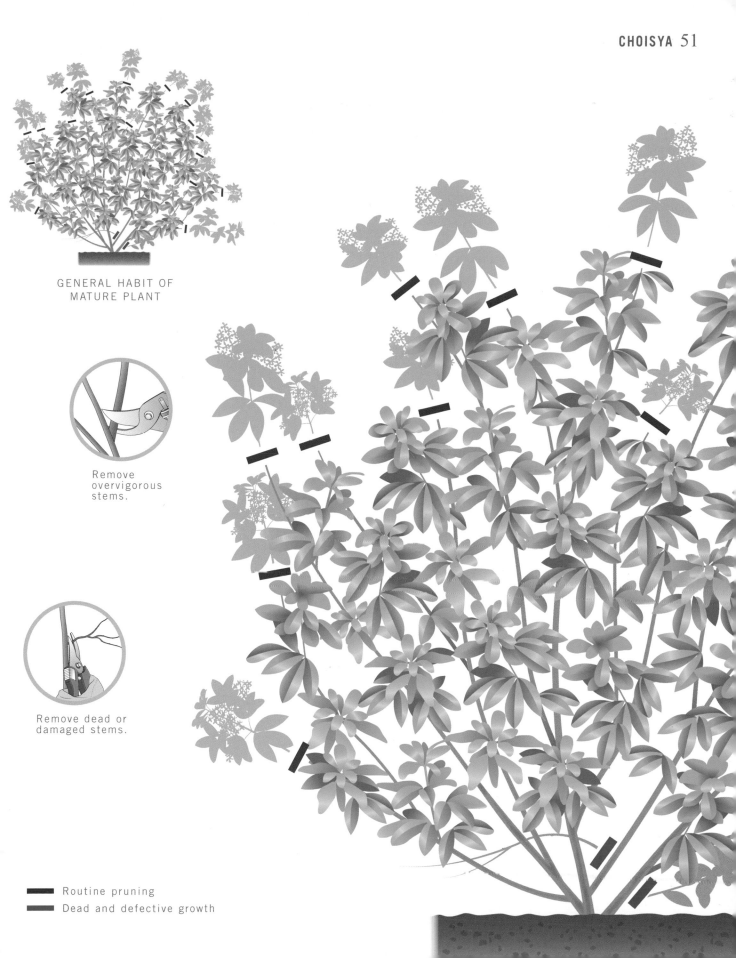

GENERAL HABIT OF
MATURE PLANT

Remove
overvigorous
stems.

Remove dead or
damaged stems.

Routine pruning
Dead and defective growth

CLEMATIS
Early-flowering clematis

If you choose carefully, it is possible to have a clematis in flower in your garden just about every month of the year, even in the depths of winter.

WHY PRUNE?
To restrict the plant's height and to encourage it to develop an open habit of growth.

PRUNING TIPS
- Start pruning as soon as possible after flowering to avoid losing next year's flowers.
- Remove older shoots with a saw because long-handled pruners (loppers) will easily crush the stems.

WHEN TO PRUNE MOST SPECIES
Late spring or early summer

PLANTS PRUNED THIS WAY
- *Clematis armandii* and cvs.: in late spring or early summer, after flowering
- *Clematis alpina* and cvs.: in late spring or early summer, after flowering
- *Clematis macropetala* and cvs.: in late spring or early summer, after flowering
- *Clematis terniflora*: in early spring, before flowering
- *Clematis montana*: in midspring, after flowering

WHICH TOOLS
- Hand pruners
- Pruning saw

FORMATIVE PRUNING

Young plants should be pruned to encourage a bushy habit with strong shoots emerging from soil level. In the first spring after planting, cut out any weak or damaged growth. Then cut back all strong, healthy stems to 12in (30cm) above ground level. The following spring cut back all shoots to 3ft (1m) above ground level.

ROUTINE PRUNING

These plants can perform reasonably well without regular pruning, but for the best possible performance they should be trimmed annually to stay tidy and to maintain a well-balanced framework of old and new growth. In early summer, immediately after flowering, cut back the old flower-bearing stems to a strong pair of buds, especially where the growth has become dense and congested or if the plant has outgrown its allotted space.

REMEDIAL PRUNING

Early-flowering clematis can become thick and congested as they age, producing few flowers. This can be overcome by hard pruning, although the following season's flowers may be lost. Cut out any dead or damaged shoots in early spring. Cut the remaining shoots back to within 2–3in (5–7cm) of ground level to encourage new shoots to replace the ones that have been removed. The following year, completely remove any thin or weak shoots. Prune out the three or four remaining old stems close to ground level.

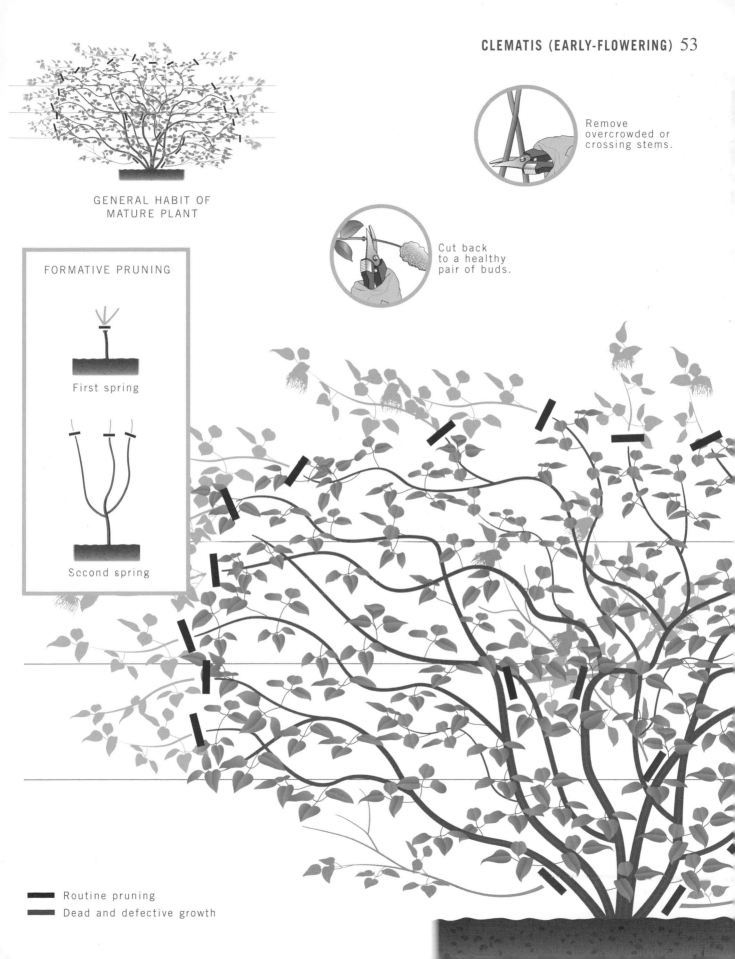

GENERAL HABIT OF
MATURE PLANT

Remove
overcrowded or
crossing stems.

Cut back
to a healthy
pair of buds.

FORMATIVE PRUNING

First spring

Second spring

Routine pruning

Dead and defective growth

CLEMATIS
Midseason-flowering clematis

It is this group of plants—the large-flowered hybrids with their big, decorative blooms covering fences, walls, and other structures—that has helped earn clematis the title "Queen of Climbers."

WHY PRUNE?

To encourage the formation of replacement shoots and to extend the flowering period.

PRUNING TIPS

- Start pruning before the new shoots form to avoid losing next year's flowers.
- Remove older shoots with a pair of long-handled pruners (loppers).

WHEN TO PRUNE MOST SPECIES

Late winter or early spring

PLANTS PRUNED THIS WAY

- *Clematis* 'Proteus': in early spring, as the buds swell
- *Clematis* 'Nelly Moser': in early spring, as the buds swell
- *Clematis* 'Vyvyan Pennell': in early spring, as the buds swell
- *Clematis* 'H.F. Young': in early spring, as the buds swell

WHICH TOOLS

- Hand pruners
- Pruning saw
- Knife

FORMATIVE PRUNING

Young plants should be pruned to encourage formation of a multistemmed plant with strong shoots emerging from soil level. In the first spring after planting, cut out any weak or damaged growth. Then cut back all strong, healthy stems to 12in (30cm) above ground level. The following spring, cut back all shoots to 3ft (1m) above ground level.

ROUTINE PRUNING

These plants can perform reasonably well without regular pruning, but they tend to produce lots of small, poor flowers if they are left completely unpruned. For best results, they should be pruned annually to stay tidy and to maintain a well-balanced framework of old and new growth. In late winter or early spring, remove any dead and weak stems. Shorten the remaining stems by 6–10in (15–25cm), cutting back to a pair of strong, healthy buds. Cutting some of these remaining shoots back by about 18in (45cm) from the tip will slightly delay their growth, and they will flower later, extending the flowering period. Tie in all remaining growths after the pruning is finished.

REMEDIAL PRUNING

This group of plants will naturally become thick and overcrowded as they age, producing thin, weak, straggly stems and few flowers, especially if the pruning has been neglected. This can be overcome by hard pruning, although the following season's flowers may be lost. On plants that have been neglected, remove any old, damaged, or diseased stems. Cut back the remaining shoots to a healthy pair of buds within 6in (15cm) of soil level. The following year, completely remove any thin or weak shoots. Shorten the remaining stems by 6–10in (15–25cm), cutting back to a pair of strong, healthy buds.

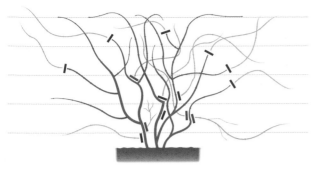

GENERAL HABIT OF
MATURE PLANT

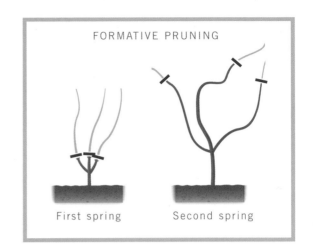

FORMATIVE PRUNING

First spring

Second spring

Cut back
to a healthy
pair of buds.

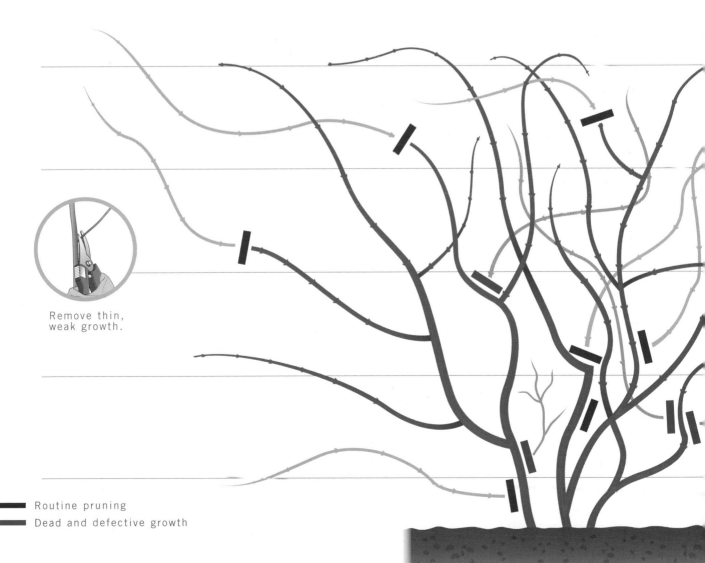

Remove thin,
weak growth.

━━ Routine pruning
━━ Dead and defective growth

CLEMATIS
Late-flowering clematis

This group includes some large-flowered cultivars as well as late-flowering species and their related cultivars.

WHY PRUNE?
To restrict the plant's height and to encourage it to develop more flowers lower down.

PRUNING TIPS
- Start pruning before the new shoots form to avoid losing the current year's flowers.
- Remove older shoots with a pair of long-handled pruners (loppers).

WHEN TO PRUNE MOST SPECIES
Late winter or early spring

PLANTS PRUNED THIS WAY
- *Clematis* 'Ville de Lyon': in late winter or early spring, as the buds swell
- *Clematis* 'Jackmanii': in late winter or early spring, as the buds swell
- *Clematis viticella* and cvs.: in late winter or early spring, as the buds swell
- *Clematis texensis* and cvs.: in late winter or early spring, as the buds swell

WHICH TOOLS
- Hand pruners
- Pruning saw

FORMATIVE PRUNING
Young plants should be pruned to encourage a bushy shape with strong shoots emerging from soil level. In the first spring after planting, prune any weak or damaged growth and cut back all strong, healthy stems to 12in (30cm) above ground level.

ROUTINE PRUNING
If they are to flower well, these clematis need regular annual pruning to remove the old wood that would otherwise gradually develop and to encourage production of new flower-bearing shoots. In early spring, completely remove any dead or damaged stems. Cut back the old flower-bearing stems to a pair of strong, healthy buds 6–8in (15–20cm) above ground level. Carefully tie in the new shoots (they are brittle) when they are about 12in (30cm) long.

REMEDIAL PRUNING
These plants should be pruned annually if they are to grow well. If they are neglected, they develop into a thicket of thin, weak, straggly stems that produce few flowers and make the plant susceptible to pests and diseases. If they have been neglected for a long time, it is usually easier to replace the plant altogether. Cut back plants that have been left unpruned for a few years to a healthy pair of buds within 6in (15cm) of ground level. Completely remove the old plant in late winter or early spring, and take care to replace the surrounding soil before planting a new, young plant. Cut the shoots back to within 2–3in (5–7cm) of ground level to encourage strong, healthy shoots.

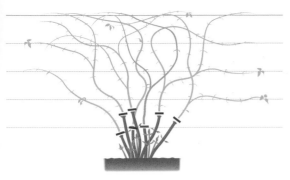

GENERAL HABIT OF
MATURE PLANT

FORMATIVE PRUNING

First spring

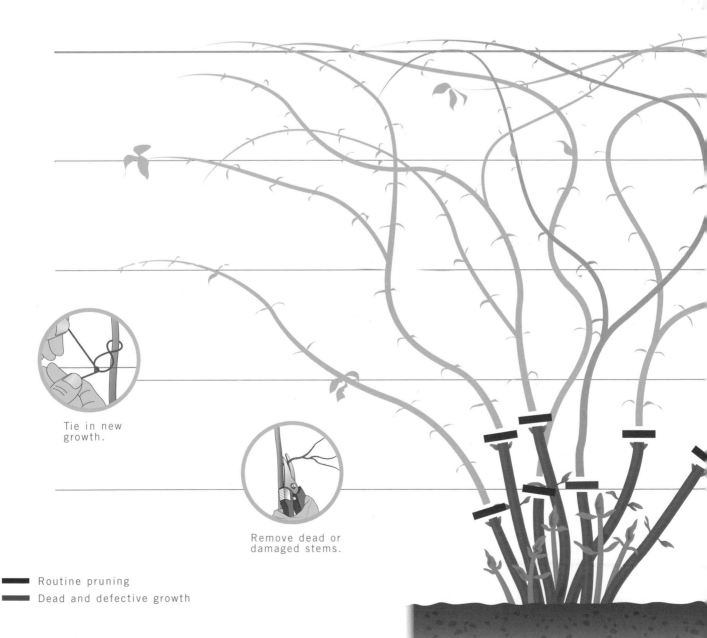

Tie in new
growth.

Remove dead or
damaged stems.

▬ Routine pruning
▬ Dead and defective growth

CORNUS ALBA AND CORNUS SERICEA

Redtwig dogwood, red-osier dogwood

The dogwoods are among the easiest garden shrubs you can grow—and their stems, leaves, and flowers provide year-round interest.

FORMATIVE PRUNING

Prune to form a multistemmed plant, with strong shoots emerging close to ground level. Plants can be cut back hard—to within 6in (15cm)—after planting in winter or early spring to encourage development of new shoots from the base.

ROUTINE PRUNING

For the most attractive winter colors, dogwoods need regular annual pruning to remove the older wood and encourage production of new shoots. At the same time, weak, thin, and diseased shoots should be removed. In early to midspring, as new growth begins, cut back one-third of the stems as close to the old branch framework as possible, leaving 1–2in (2.5–5cm) stubs of growth from which the new shoots will emerge. When the old stubs of growth become overcrowded, remove them with a small pruning saw.

REMEDIAL PRUNING

When they are left unpruned, dogwoods become overcrowded. A mass of thin, weak, straggly, poorly colored stems makes the plants susceptible to pests and diseases. This can be overcome with hard pruning. In winter, cut back all of the old stems as close to the old branch framework as possible, using a saw if necessary and leaving 1–2in (2.5–5cm) stubs of growth from which the new shoots will emerge. In late spring, completely remove any thin or weak shoots.

WHY PRUNE?
To promote the production of new, brightly colored shoots.

PRUNING TIPS
Cut close to the buds to prevent dieback.

WHEN TO PRUNE MOST SPECIES
Early or midspring

PLANTS PRUNED THIS WAY
- *Cornus alba* and cvs.: in early or midspring
- *Cornus sericea* and cvs.: in early or midspring
- *Cornus sanguinea* and cvs.: in early or midspring

WHICH TOOLS
- Hand pruners
- Long-handled pruners (loppers)
- Pruning saw

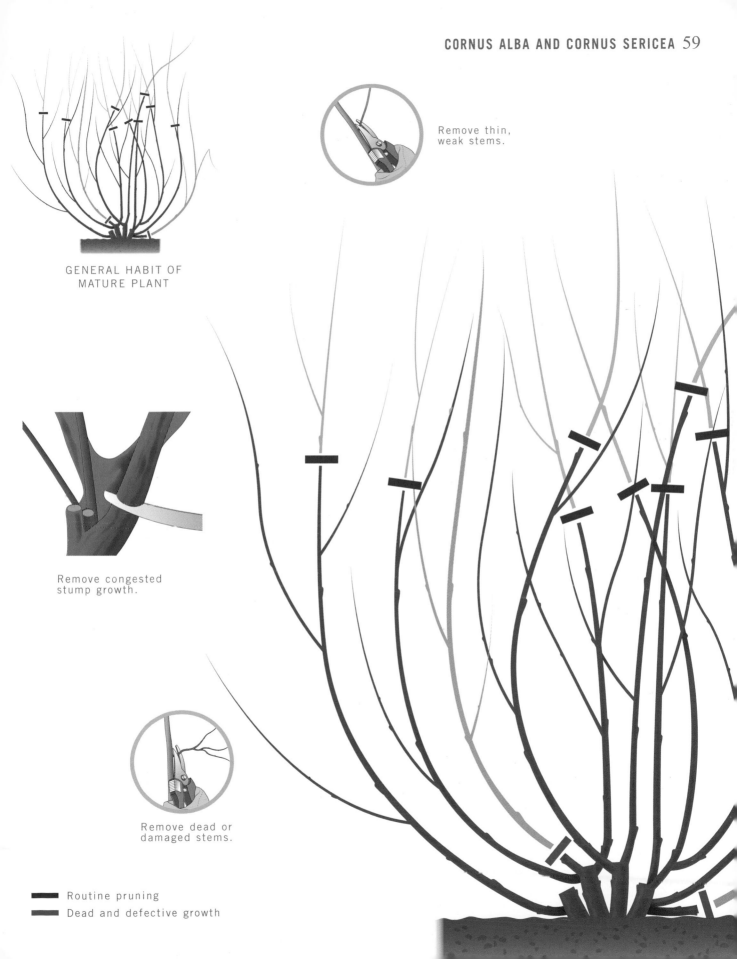

GENERAL HABIT OF
MATURE PLANT

Remove thin,
weak stems.

Remove congested
stump growth.

Remove dead or
damaged stems.

Routine pruning
Dead and defective growth

COTINUS

Smoke bush, Venetian sumac

The common name smoke bush describes the clusters of tiny flowers that sometimes make you rub your eyes and look at this shrub twice to see if it really does have a fire behind it or if the "smoke" is drifting on the wind.

WHY PRUNE?

No regular pruning is required but cutting the plant back hard for foliage effect is an option.

PRUNING TIPS

Regular hard pruning will induce extra large leaves to grow, but plants treated in this manner will not flower.

WHEN TO PRUNE MOST SPECIES

Early spring

PLANTS PRUNED THIS WAY

- *Cotinus coggygria* and cvs.: in early spring, but only if required
- *Cotinus obovatus* and cvs.: in early spring, but only if required

WHICH TOOLS

- Hand pruners
- Long-handled pruners (loppers)
- Pruning saw

FORMATIVE PRUNING

Prune young plants to encourage them to grow bushy, with strong shoots emerging from just above soil level. In spring, just before the new growth starts, cut out any thin, weak growth or damaged shoots. Cut the remaining shoots back to three or four buds above ground level.

ROUTINE PRUNING

If they are to flower well, these plants are best left unpruned, although you should cut out any overcrowded, damaged, or rubbing shoots to create a multibranched plant and prevent it from becoming too tall, straggly, and unmanageable. Cut off the old flower stalks in spring, before the new growth starts. Cut out any thin, straggly growths, because they rarely produce good flowers and often harbor pests and diseases. An alternative method to promote purple foliage is to cut the entire plant to within 12in (30cm) of the ground. The leaves will grow in larger, and the plant will act as a colorful foliage accent.

REMEDIAL PRUNING

These shrubs often produce long, bare shoots and become open and rangy as they age. Remedial pruning is best done over two years. In the first year, cut half of the main shoots back to within 6–8in (15–20cm) of soil level. Cut down to ground level any thin, weak shoots. In the second year, cut the remaining old stems back to 6–8in (15–20cm) above ground level. Remove any thin, spindly shoots that developed from the previous year's pruning.

GENERAL HABIT OF
MATURE PLANT

Remove
dead
flowers.

Remove thin,
weak growth.

Remove overcrowded
or crossing stems.

▬ Routine pruning
▬ Dead and defective growth

COTONEASTER
(deciduous species)
Cotoneaster

Cotoneasters are hardy, adaptable plants, providing structure and form in the garden as well as an excellent display of flowers in spring and summer and small, berrylike fruits throughout fall and long into winter.

FORMATIVE PRUNING

Prune young plants to encourage them to become multistemmed, with a framework of about six strong, evenly spaced shoots emerging close to ground level. In the first spring after planting, remove any dead or damaged shoots. Cut the remaining stems back to 6–8in (15–20cm) above ground level. As these stems develop, remove any branches crossing through the middle of the shrub.

ROUTINE PRUNING

Established plants need little routine pruning and will flower and fruit for many years without any pruning at all. It may only be necessary to remove dead or damaged shoots and prune to prevent congestion in the center of the plant. Remove dead or damaged stems, cutting back to healthy growth, and prune out any branches that cross through the middle of the plant. Old or nonproductive shoots can be cut down to within 2–3in (5–7cm) of ground level and a new shoot allowed to grow as a replacement.

REMEDIAL PRUNING

Cotoneasters often become bare and leggy at the base. They respond well to remedial pruning, but this works better if it is phased over two years rather than cutting back the plant in one operation. In winter, before new growth starts, cut the thickest branches down to about 2ft (60cm) above ground level. The following year, cut any remaining old branches down to the same height. You may need to thin out new shoots to prevent overcrowding.

WHY PRUNE?

To maintain even growth and to promote flowering and fruiting.

PRUNING TIPS

Prune only when absolutely necessary.

WHEN TO PRUNE MOST SPECIES

Late winter

PLANTS PRUNED THIS WAY

- *Cotoneaster adpressus* and cvs.: in late winter, before new growth starts
- *Cotoneaster apiculatus* and cvs.: in late winter, before new growth starts
- *Cotoneaster divaricatus* and cvs.: in late winter, before new growth starts
- *Cotoneaster horizontalis* and cvs.: in late winter, before new growth starts
- *Cotoneaster multiflorus* and cvs.: in late winter, before new growth starts
- *Cotoneaster simonsii* and cvs.: in late winter, before new growth starts

WHICH TOOLS

- Hand pruners
- Long-handled pruners (loppers)
- Pruning saw

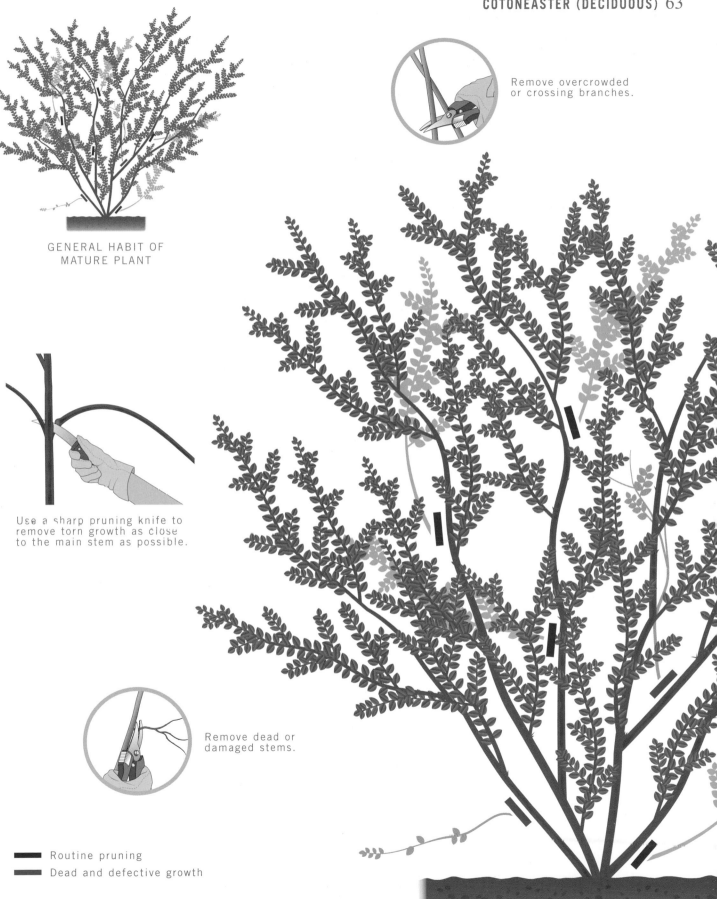

GENERAL HABIT OF
MATURE PLANT

Remove overcrowded
or crossing branches.

Use a sharp pruning knife to
remove torn growth as close
to the main stem as possible.

Remove dead or
damaged stems.

Routine pruning
Dead and defective growth

COTONEASTER
(evergreen species)
Cotoneaster

These hardy, adaptable plants bring structure and form to a garden as well as an excellent display of flowers in spring and summer and small, berrylike fruits in the fall and long into winter.

WHY PRUNE?
To maintain an open habit and to create a framework of strong branches.

PRUNING TIPS
Look out for fireblight, a serious bacterial disease (symptoms include the death of new shoots and scorched-looking flowers and leaves), and prune out and burn affected growths immediately.

WHEN TO PRUNE MOST SPECIES
Winter or midspring

PLANTS PRUNED THIS WAY
- *Cotoneaster* 'Cornubia': in winter or midspring
- *Cotoneaster dammeri* and cvs.: in winter or midspring
- *Cotoneaster lacteus* and cvs.: in winter or midspring
- *Cotoneaster salicifolius* and cvs.: in winter or midspring

WHICH TOOLS
- Hand pruners
- Long-handled pruners (loppers)
- Pruning saw

FORMATIVE PRUNING

Prune young plants to encourage them to become multistemmed, with a framework of about six strong shoots forming close to ground level. In the first spring after planting, remove any dead or damaged stems. Cut the remaining stems back to 6–8in (15–20cm) above ground level. As these stems develop, cut out any branches that cross through the middle of the shrub.

ROUTINE PRUNING

Once established, these plants need little routine pruning and will flower and fruit for many years without any pruning at all. Some pruning may be necessary to prevent the plant from becoming congested in the center. Remove any dead or damaged stems, cutting back to healthy growth. Prune out any branches that cross through the middle of the plant. Spreading species and cultivars may need yearly pruning to keep them within their alloted space.

REMEDIAL PRUNING

As they age, these plants often become bare and leggy at the base, particularly if they have been neglected for a number of years, but they will usually respond well to hard pruning. In winter, cut the plant back to a framework of strong shoots within 12in (30cm) above ground level. As the new growth develops, remove any thin or weak shoots, cutting back to stronger stems or to ground level.

GENERAL HABIT OF
MATURE PLANT

Remove dead and
damaged growth.

Remove
overcrowded or
crossing stems.

Routine pruning

Dead and defective growth

FICUS
Ornamental fig

These attractive evergreens, with their bold, glossy leaves, make excellent specimen plants in a container or border. Where hardy, they provide useful structure in the winter garden when other plants are bare.

WHY PRUNE?

To maintain shape and to keep the plant within its allotted space.

PRUNING TIPS

Take care not to get sap on exposed skin; some people may suffer a phytochemical reaction in hot, humid weather, and blisters may occur.

WHEN TO PRUNE MOST SPECIES

Late winter or early spring

PLANTS PRUNED THIS WAY

- *Ficus benjamina*: in late winter or early spring
- *Ficus elastica*: in late winter or early spring
- *Ficus lyrata*: in late winter or early spring
- *Ficus macrophylla*: in late winter or early spring

WHICH TOOLS

- Hand pruners
- Long-handled pruners (loppers)
- Pruning saw
- Thick gloves

FORMATIVE PRUNING

Prune young plants to encourage them to become bushy and well-structured, with a central main stem and plenty of branches originating from it. Remove the top 4–6in (10–15cm) of the main stem to encourage branching along its length. In spring, cut any weak, leggy shoots back to about two-thirds. Remove the end third of any long, straggly shoots.

ROUTINE PRUNING

Ornamental figs will grow well for many years with little or no pruning, but shortening the previous season's growth by about one-quarter in late winter or early spring will encourage the development of a bushy, balanced plant with a good framework of branches. This is also a good way of keeping the plant from getting too leggy. In spring, shorten by one-third any overly vigorous shoots to prevent the plant from becoming unbalanced and lopsided.

REMEDIAL PRUNING

These plants can be cut back quite severely—often back to the main framework of branches—to promote new growth or to overcome wind damage. Remove all of the smaller (sublateral) branches and cut the framework branches back to within 18in (45cm) of the main stem.

GENERAL HABIT OF
MATURE PLANT

Remove dead or
damaged stems.

Shorten
overvigorous
stems.

Routine pruning
Dead and defective growth

FORSYTHIA

Forsythia

A welcome harbinger of spring, the flowers of this popular and easy-to-grow shrub are borne on usually bare stems.

WHY PRUNE?

To restrict the plant's height and to encourage it to develop an open habit of growth.

PRUNING TIPS

- Start pruning as soon as possible after flowering to avoid losing next year's flowers.
- Remove older shoots with a saw because long-handled pruners (loppers) will easily crush the stems.

WHEN TO PRUNE MOST SPECIES

Late spring or early summer

PLANTS PRUNED THIS WAY

- *Forsythia ×intermedia*: in late spring or early summer
- *Forsythia ovata*: in late spring or early summer
- *Forsythia suspensa*: in late spring or early summer
- *Deutzia gracilis* and cvs.: in late spring or early summer
- *Deutzia scabra* and cvs.: in late spring or early summer

WHICH TOOLS

- Hand pruners
- Pruning saw

FORMATIVE PRUNING

Young plants should be pruned to encourage a bushy shape, with strong shoots emerging from soil level. After planting, cut out any weak or damaged growth. Lightly pinch back the remaining shoots to about two-thirds of their length to encourage new shoots from the base of the plant as it becomes established.

ROUTINE PRUNING

If they are to flower well, forsythias need regular annual pruning to remove the old wood that would gradually develop and to encourage production of new flower-bearing shoots. Immediately after flowering, cut back all old flower-bearing stems at least halfway along their length to just above a healthy bud or to a well-placed new sideshoot. The old flower-bearing shoots of golden bell (*Forsythia suspensa*) should be pruned back to within two buds of their base. Do this in late spring or early summer to give the maximum period of growth to produce a good display of flowers the following year. On mature shrubs, try to remove about one-quarter to one-fifth of the old stems each year to allow in light and make room for new shoots to develop.

REMEDIAL PRUNING

Forsythia shrubs will naturally become dense and overcrowded as they age, and the thicket of thin, weak, straggly stems will produce few flowers and make the plant susceptible to pests and diseases. This can be overcome by hard pruning, which must be done in stages over two or three years. Leaving just three or four strong stems, in late winter or early spring cut all other shoots back to within 2–3in (5–7cm) of ground level to encourage new replacement shoots to develop. The following year, completely remove any thin or weak shoots. Prune out the three or four remaining old stems, cutting close to ground level.

GENERAL HABIT OF
MATURE PLANT

Remedial pruning: Cut out
old stems out just above
a replacement shoot.

Cut back to a
healthy bud.

▬ Routine pruning
▬ Dead and defective growth

FREMONTODENDRON
Flannel bush

An outstanding wall shrub for a warm, sunny position, the fremontodendron will produce large, saucer-shaped, bright yellow flowers from late spring until midfall.

WHY PRUNE?

To maintain a bushy habit and a framework of strong branches.

PRUNING TIPS

Wear gloves and a face mask, because the stems and young leaves are covered with irritating hairs.

WHEN TO PRUNE MOST SPECIES

Midsummer

PLANTS PRUNED THIS WAY

- *Fremontodendron californicum* and cvs.: in midsummer, after the first flush of flowers
- *Fremontodendron mexicanum* and cvs.: in midsummer, after the first flush of flowers

WHICH TOOLS

- Hand pruners
- Long-handled pruners (loppers)
- Gloves
- Face mask

FORMATIVE PRUNING

Prune young plants to encourage them to grow bushy and well-structured, with a central main stem and plenty of branches originating from it. Remove the top 4–6in (10–15cm) of the main stem to encourage branching along its length. In spring, cut any weak, leggy shoots back to two or three buds. Remove the end third of any long, straggly shoots.

ROUTINE PRUNING

Fremontodendron will grow well for many years with little or no pruning, but shortening the previous season's growth by about one-quarter in summer, immediately after the first flush of flowers, will produce a bushy, free-flowering plant. This is also a good way to keep the plant from getting too bare and leggy. In summer, cut the flower-bearing shoots back to within three to five buds of the old wood to encourage the plant to develop many short, flowering stems. In summer, shorten by one-third any overly vigorous shoots so that the plant does not become unbalanced and lopsided.

REMEDIAL PRUNING

These plants may become bare at the base, but they do not respond well to severe pruning, and it is better to replace an old plant than to attempt to revive it. Dig up the old plant and replace it.

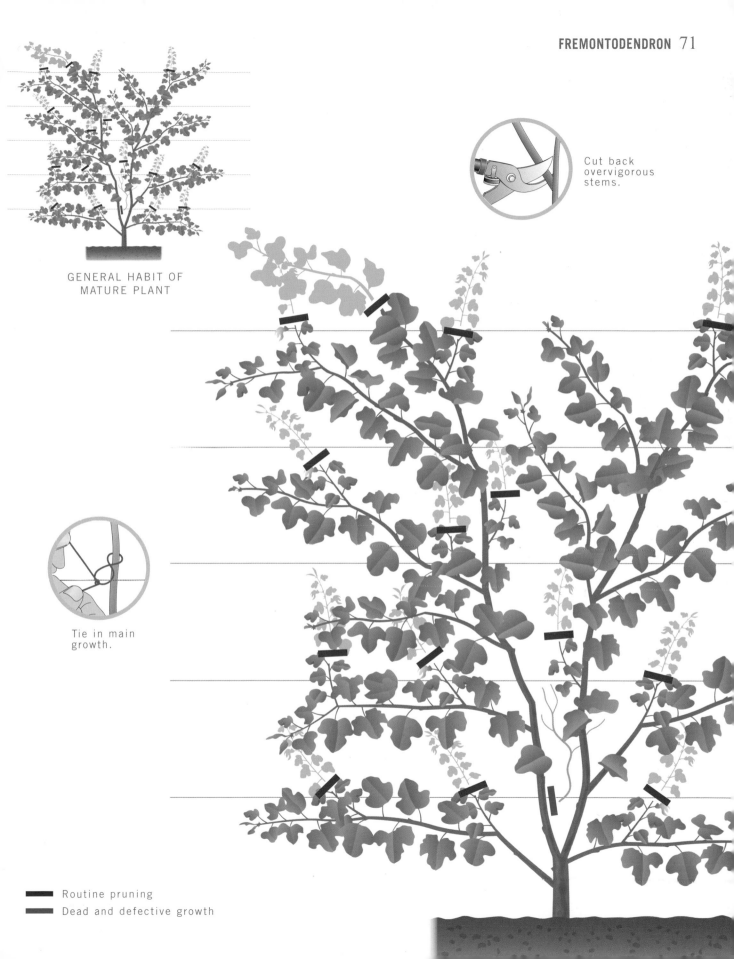

GENERAL HABIT OF
MATURE PLANT

Cut back
overvigorous
stems.

Tie in main
growth.

Routine pruning

Dead and defective growth

FUCHSIA
Lady's eardrops

Outdoor fuchsias are among the most reliable flowering shrubs you can plant in your garden. They will flower from early summer until the frosts stop them, and as long as they are watered regularly, they will grow in most conditions.

WHY PRUNE?
To encourage the development of healthy new shoots and regular flowers.

PRUNING TIPS
Prune after the last spring frost.

WHEN TO PRUNE MOST SPECIES
Early spring

PLANTS PRUNED THIS WAY
- *Fuchsia magellanica*: in early spring, once growth has started
- *Fuchsia* 'Mrs. Popple': in early spring, once growth has started
- *Fuchsia* 'Ricartonii': in early spring, once growth has started

WHICH TOOLS
- Hand pruners
- Long-handled pruners (loppers)

FORMATIVE PRUNING
Prune young plants to encourage them to grow bushy, with plenty of strong, vigorous shoots emerging from soil level. After planting, remove any weak or damaged growth. Cut the remaining shoots back to about one-third of their length to encourage the development of new shoots from the base of the plant.

ROUTINE PRUNING
Regular pruning will encourage the development of strong, young, flower-bearing stems or lateral branches, but wait until the new growth has started so that you notice any frost-damaged shoots. Cut all the main stems back to about 12in (30cm) above ground level. Prune back all lateral shoots to a strong pair of buds close to the main stem.

REMEDIAL PRUNING
If fuchsias are left unpruned for a number of years, they produce many weak, short, thin stems and much smaller flowers. They also become bare at the base of the stems. In spring, cut all the stems back to within 2–3in (5–7cm) of ground level, and in summer remove up to about one-third of the weakest and thinnest shoots to prevent overcrowding.

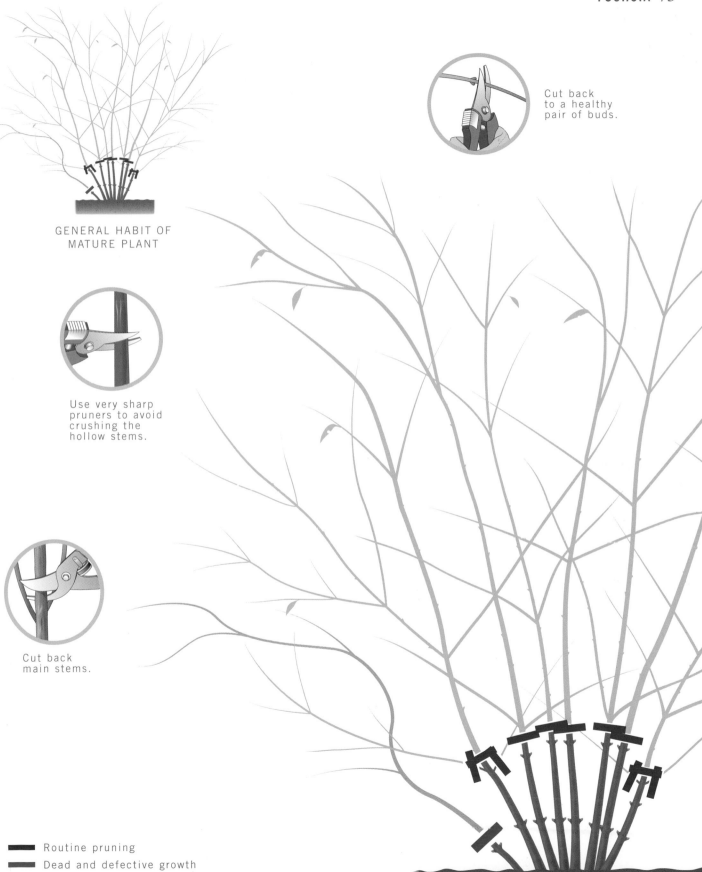

Cut back
to a healthy
pair of buds.

GENERAL HABIT OF
MATURE PLANT

Use very sharp
pruners to avoid
crushing the
hollow stems.

Cut back
main stems.

■ Routine pruning
■ Dead and defective growth

HEDERA

Common ivy, climbing ivy

Its numerous cultivars make ivy one of the most useful of all climbers, whether you are covering horizontal or vertical surfaces.

WHY PRUNE?
To control plant growth and to encourage even coverage of the allotted area.

PRUNING TIPS
Before pruning, spray the plants with a garden hose to wash away the dust.

WHEN TO PRUNE MOST SPECIES
Early spring

PLANTS PRUNED THIS WAY
- *Hedera canariensis* and cvs.: in early spring and throughout the season as needed
- *Hedera colchica* and cvs.: in early spring and throughout the season as needed
- *Hedera helix* and cvs.: in early spring and throughout the season as needed
- *Parthenocissus quinquefolia* and cvs.: in fall or early winter, when stems are visible
- *Parthenocissus tricuspidata* and cvs.: in fall or early winter, when stems are visible

WHICH TOOLS
- Hand pruners
- Long-handled pruners (loppers)
- Pruning saw

FORMATIVE PRUNING

Try to develop a multistemmed plant, with strong shoots emerging close to ground level. In the first spring after planting, cut the shoots back by removing about one-third of their length.

ROUTINE PRUNING

Pruning will keep the plant within its allotted space and keep it from climbing up valued trees. Pinch off the tips to encourage them to branch and provide better coverage. Pruning may also be necessary to trim back any shoots that are growing out from the support. In spring, before new growth starts, prune all shoots that are growing beyond their allotted space, cutting back to 2ft (60cm) inside the area to allow the shoots to branch. Cut all vigorous, outward-facing growth back to its point of origin.

REMEDIAL PRUNING

Renovate plants that are totally overgrown and out of control, especially when they become bare at the base, with severe pruning. In spring, cut all the shoots back to within 2ft (60cm) of ground level. Train in the new shoots as they emerge.

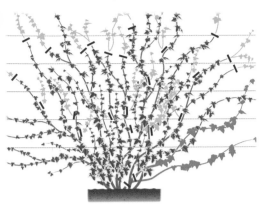

GENERAL HABIT OF
MATURE PLANT

Ivy leaves alter in shape
and color as they mature.
Remove adult growth if
you find it unattractive.

Remove
overvigorous
stems.

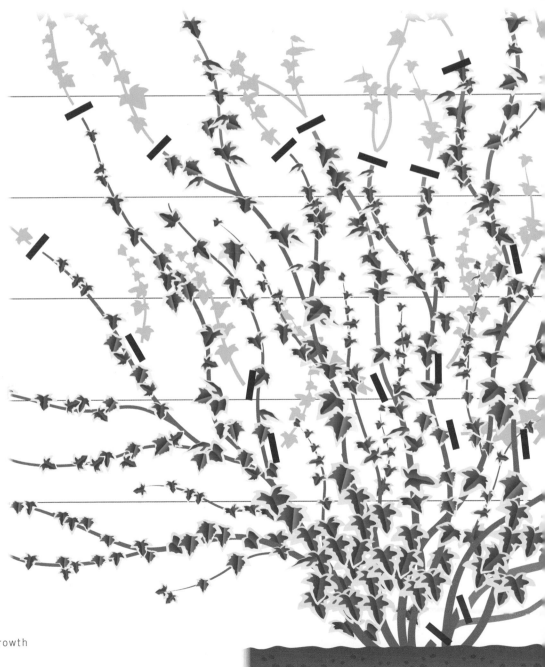

▬▬ Routine pruning

▬▬ Dead and defective growth

HIBISCUS

Rose mallow, tree hollyhock

Hibiscus are grown for their large, attractive, colorful blooms, which are produced on the new growth in late summer and early fall.

WHY PRUNE?
To keep the plant healthy and flowering regularly.

PRUNING TIPS
Prune as the plant starts to grow in spring so that any dead or dying shoots are easily seen.

WHEN TO PRUNE MOST SPECIES
Late winter or early spring

PLANTS PRUNED THIS WAY
• *Hibiscus rosa-sinensis* and cvs.: in late winter or early spring, as new growth begins
• *Hibiscus syriacus* and cvs.: in late winter or early spring, as new growth begins

WHICH TOOLS
• Hand pruners
• Long-handled pruners (loppers)

FORMATIVE PRUNING
Prune young plants to encourage them to develop a bushy habit, with strong shoots emerging from just above ground level. After planting, cut out any weak or damaged growth. Cut the remaining shoots back to about half their length to encourage new shoots to develop from the base of the plant.

ROUTINE PRUNING
These plants need little regular pruning, although you need to remove weak or dead growth and to cut back any very vigorous shoots, which may cause the plant to become lopsided. Pinch off the tips of any thin, weak shoots by cutting them back to half their length. Remove any dead or dying shoots, cutting back cleanly to healthy growth.

REMEDIAL PRUNING
It may be necessary to rebalance a one-sided plant, to reduce overall plant size to prevent damage to brittle root systems, and to remove any dead shoots to prevent fungal attacks. Completely remove older branches. Cut the remaining branches back by two-thirds of their original length.

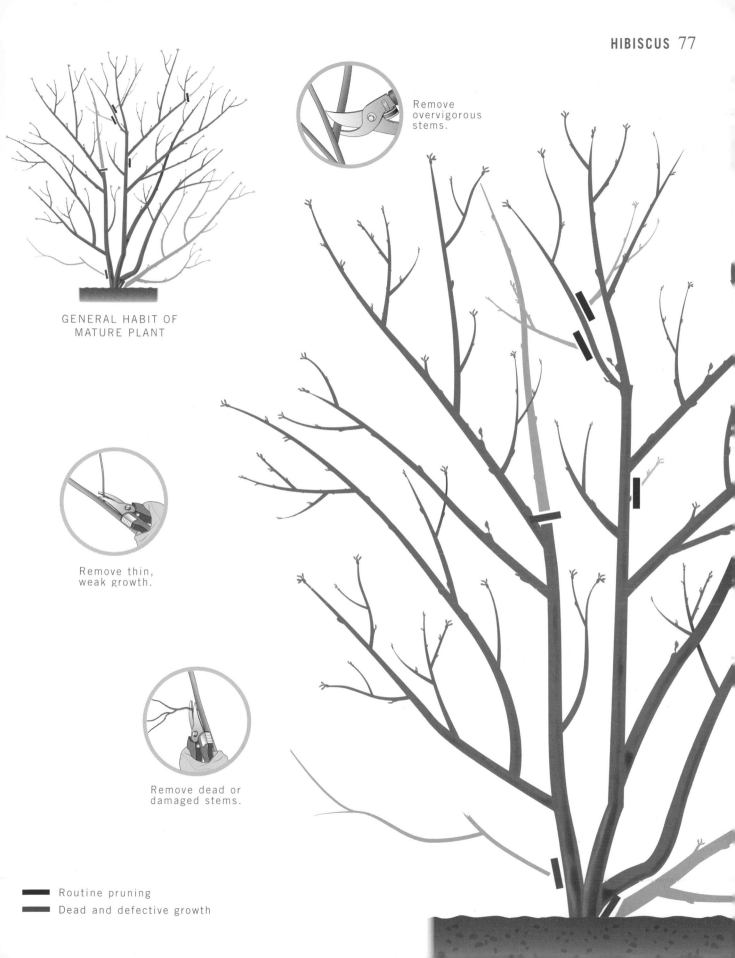

GENERAL HABIT OF
MATURE PLANT

Remove
overvigorous
stems.

Remove thin,
weak growth.

Remove dead or
damaged stems.

■ Routine pruning
■ Dead and defective growth

HYDRANGEA

Shrubby hydrangea, common hydrangea

The massed flowers of hydrangeas are familiar sights in all but the very coldest of gardens, bringing delicate shades from summer to early winter.

WHY PRUNE?

To improve flower size and quality and to encourage the plant to develop an open, balanced shape.

PRUNING TIPS

Use sharp tools so that you do not accidentally split the stems.

WHEN TO PRUNE MOST SPECIES

Early spring

PLANTS PRUNED THIS WAY

- *Hydrangea arborescens* and cvs.: in spring, as new growth starts
- *Hydrangea paniculata* and cvs.: in spring, as new growth starts
- *Hydrangea quercifolia* and cvs.: in spring, as new growth starts
- *Hydrangea macrophylla* and cvs.: in late summer, after flowering
- *Hydrangea serrata* and cvs.: in late summer, after flowering

WHICH TOOLS

- Hand pruners
- Long-handled pruners (loppers)
- Pruning saw

FORMATIVE PRUNING

Prune young plants to encourage them to develop a bushy habit, with strong shoots emerging from just at or above ground level. After planting, cut out any weak or damaged growth. Lightly pinch off the remaining shoots to about two-thirds of their length so new shoots can emerge from the base of the plant.

ROUTINE PRUNING

Hydrangeas need regular pruning if they are to flower well. It is important to remove the old wood, which would otherwise gradually accumulate. In spring, prune species that bloom on new growth by shortening each shoot by about one-third, cutting back to a pair of strong, healthy buds so that there is a good display of flowers later in the year. Cut thin, spindly shoots back to ground level. Remove any shoots that are crossing and rubbing.

REMEDIAL PRUNING

Hydrangeas tend to become woody and overcrowded as they age, with lots of thin, weak, straggly stems producing fewer and fewer flowers, especially if pruning has been neglected. This can be overcome with hard pruning, although the following season's flowers may be lost. In late winter or early spring, cut the old, strong shoots back to within 4–6in (10–15cm) of ground level. Cut out any thin, weak growth so new shoots can develop.

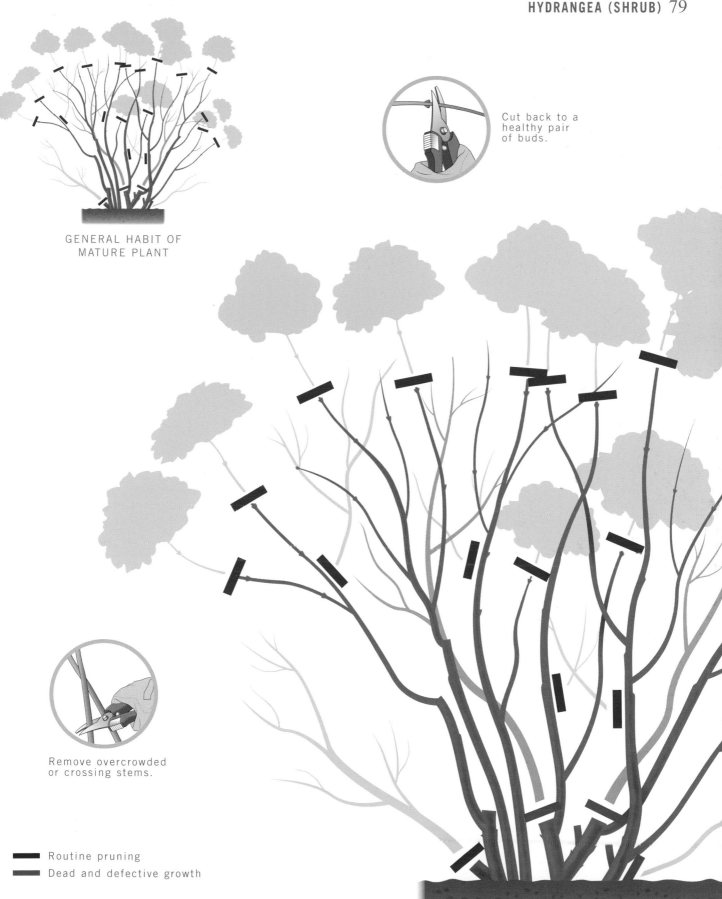

GENERAL HABIT OF
MATURE PLANT

Cut back to a
healthy pair
of buds.

Remove overcrowded
or crossing stems.

Routine pruning
Dead and defective growth

HYDRANGEA
Climbing hydrangea

Ideal plants for brightening a shady wall, climbing hydrangeas bear wonderful clusters of blooms from summer into late fall.

WHY PRUNE?

To control the plant and to encourage the production of flowers.

PRUNING TIPS

After remedial pruning, it may be two or three years before the plants start to flower again.

WHEN TO PRUNE MOST SPECIES

Late summer

PLANTS PRUNED THIS WAY

- *Akebia quinata*: in late spring, after flowering
- *Hydrangea seemannii*: in late summer, after flowering
- *Hydrangea serratifolia*: in late summer, after flowering
- *Stauntonia hexaphylla*: in late spring, after flowering

WHICH TOOLS

- Hand pruners
- Long-handled pruners (loppers)

FORMATIVE PRUNING

Young plants need little pruning because they will naturally develop a bushy habit, with strong shoots emerging from just above ground level. In the first spring after planting, cut out any weak or damaged growth. Train the new growth against the support structure.

ROUTINE PRUNING

Pruning will keep the plant within its allotted space, while pinching the tips off shoots will encourage them to branch and provide better coverage. Shoots that grow outward from their support should also be trimmed back. In late summer after the plants flower, cut back all shoots that are growing beyond their allotted space. Cut back to 2ft (60cm) inside the allotted area to allow the shoots to branch. Cut all vigorous, outward-facing growth back to two or three buds from its point of origin.

REMEDIAL PRUNING

Plants tend to become bare at the base and rather top-heavy. They produce most of the flowers on the top branches that are often out of sight. Drastic pruning will bring the plant back under control. In spring, cut all growth back to leave a framework of main stems and branches. Phase the work over two or three years.

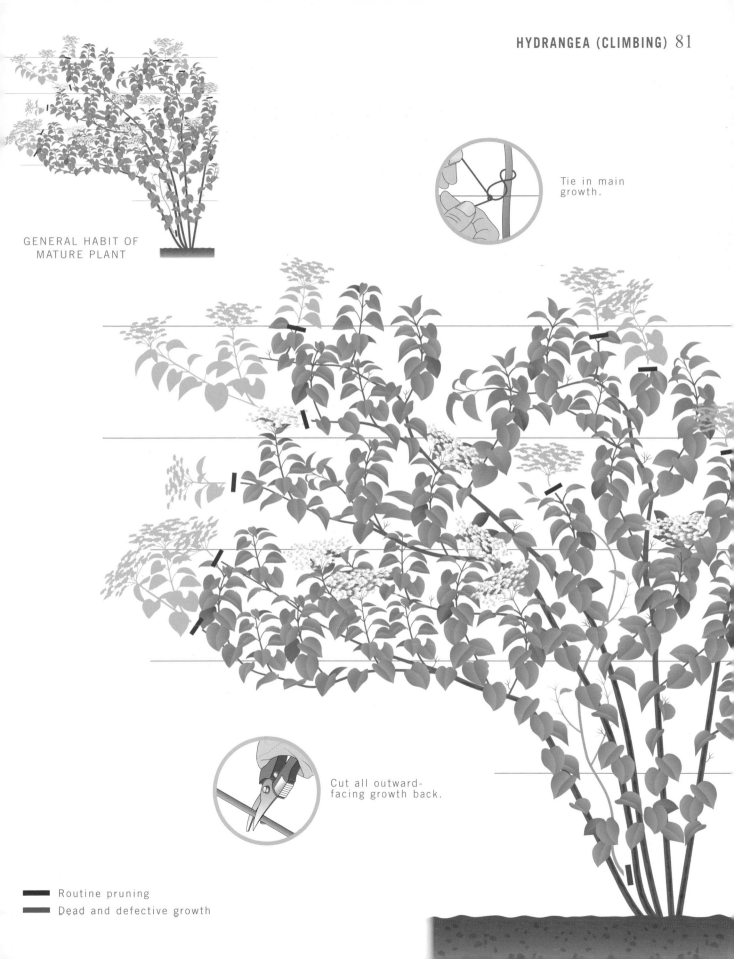

GENERAL HABIT OF
MATURE PLANT

Tie in main
growth.

Cut all outward-
facing growth back.

Routine pruning
Dead and defective growth

ILEX
Holly

One plant that everyone knows is holly, even if only because of its association with Christmas.

WHY PRUNE?
To maintain an open, balanced, well-shaped plant.

PRUNING TIPS
Don't prune in fall, because the new growth may be damaged by frosts.

WHEN TO PRUNE MOST SPECIES
Mid- or late summer

PLANTS PRUNED THIS WAY
- *Ilex aquifolium* and cvs.: in mid- or late summer
- *Ilex crenata* and cvs.: in late winter or early spring
- *Ilex glabra* and cvs.: in late winter or early spring
- *Ilex opaca* and cvs.: in mid- or late summer
- *Ilex ×altaclarensis* and cvs.: in mid- or late summer

WHICH TOOLS
- Hand pruners
- Pruning saw
- Pruning shears
- Thornproof gloves

FORMATIVE PRUNING

Hollies usually have a main stem or central leader with a series of laterals or side branches, and pruning keeps the main shoot growing strongly while encouraging the laterals to become bushy. After planting, trim back any broken or damaged growth and remove the end 2in (5cm) of growth from the sideshoots to encourage them to branch. If striving to maintain a pyramidal shape, remove any strong shoots that compete with the central leader.

ROUTINE PRUNING

Hollies grown in a tree form do not require regular pruning to keep growing well, but you can pinch off the tips when the plant is young to keep it in a desired shape. Vigorous shoots should be cut back to balance the growth and shape of the plant. In late summer, remove the tips of shoots, cutting off 2–4in (5–10cm) of growth to encourage branching. Remove any competing leaders. Prune vigorous stems by at least half their length, cutting back to just above a healthy bud or to a well-placed sideshoot. Remove any thin, weak growth from the center of the plant.

REMEDIAL PRUNING

As they age, hollies make less extension growth at the tip of each shoot, and they increase in overall size very slowly. At the same time, they often become bare and straggly at the base. Holly trees (*I. aquifolium* and *I. opaca*) are slow growing and generally do not require renovation.

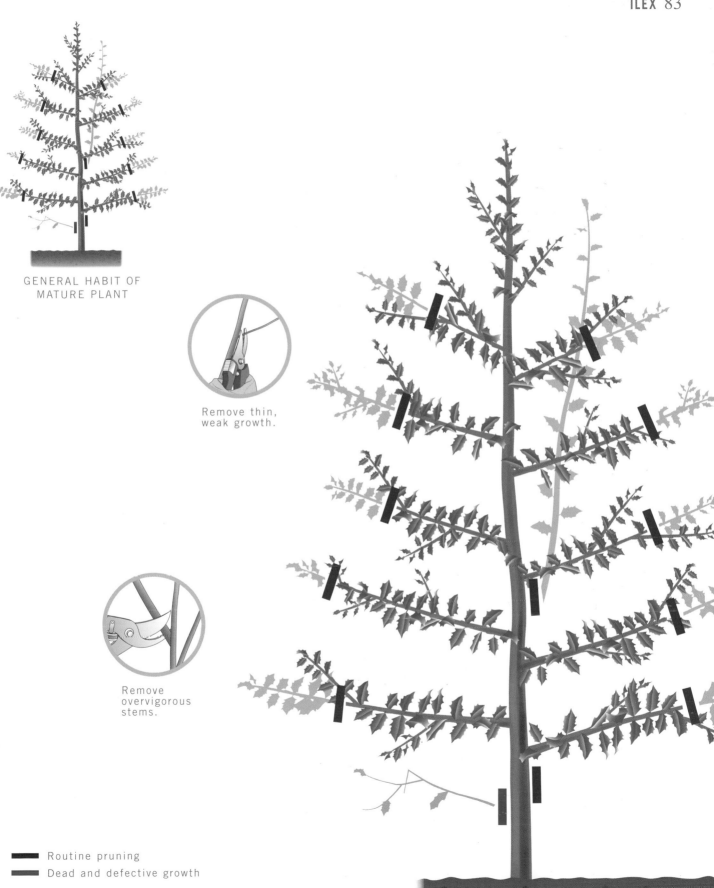

GENERAL HABIT OF
MATURE PLANT

Remove thin,
weak growth.

Remove
overvigorous
stems.

▬ Routine pruning
▬ Dead and defective growth

JASMINUM

Jasmine, jessamine

These scrambling climbers are grown for their attractive and often fragrant blooms. They make ideal screens to camouflage or hide items and parts of the garden that you would prefer to keep out of sight.

WHY PRUNE?

To maintain balanced growth and to encourage flowering.

PRUNING TIPS

Prune jasmine after flowering so that you don't remove blooming shoots.

WHEN TO PRUNE MOST SPECIES

Early spring

PLANTS PRUNED THIS WAY

- *Jasminum nudiflorum*: in spring, after flowering
- *Jasminum officinale*: in winter, after flowering
- *Jasminum polyanthum*: in summer, after flowering

WHICH TOOLS

- Hand pruners
- Long-handled pruners (loppers)

FORMATIVE PRUNING

Prune young plants to encourage them to grow bushy, with a number of strong, vigorous shoots emerging from close to soil level. In the first spring after planting, cut out any weak or damaged growth, and cut all strong, healthy stems back to about two-thirds of their original length. Train the new shoots into the support structure as they develop.

ROUTINE PRUNING

Try to produce a framework of strong, healthy shoots and encourage the formation of flower-bearing spurs. Also, prune mature plants to keep them within their allotted space. Cut the lateral flower-bearing shoots back to two or three pairs of strong buds; these will bear the current season's flowers. Remove any weak or straggly growths. To encourage branching, cut back to a strong bud any vigorous shoots that are growing out of their allotted space.

REMEDIAL PRUNING

Jasmines often become leggy and bare at the base, but they will respond well to severe pruning. In late winter or early spring, use hand pruners or long-handled pruners (loppers) to cut all the stems back to within 2ft (60cm) of ground level. This will encourage the development of new shoots. Six to eight weeks after cutting down the plant, remove all the weak, thin shoots and start to train the new replacement shoots into position on the support structure.

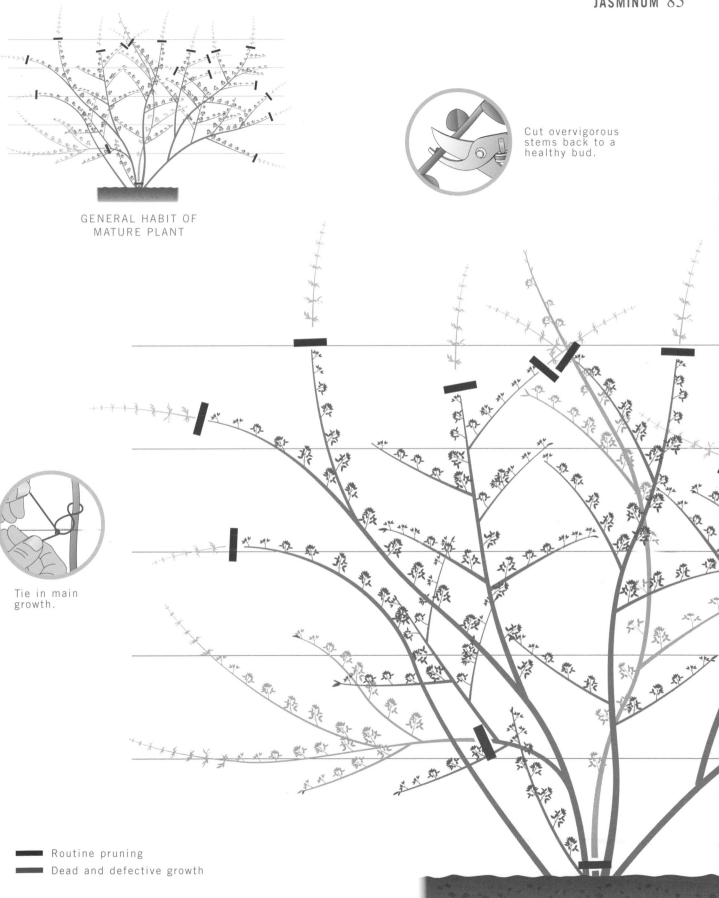

GENERAL HABIT OF
MATURE PLANT

Cut overvigorous
stems back to a
healthy bud.

Tie in main
growth.

▬ Routine pruning
▬ Dead and defective growth

LAGERSTROEMIA

Pride of India, crape myrtle

These shrubs and trees are suitable only for reliably warm gardens with hot summers, but in the right conditions they flower profusely and for long periods. As well as brightly colored flowers, they have decorative foliage and attractive peeling bark.

WHY PRUNE?

To encourage balanced growth and regular flowering.

PRUNING TIPS

Prune so that plenty of light can get into the center of the plant.

WHEN TO PRUNE MOST SPECIES

Early spring

PLANTS PRUNED THIS WAY

- *Lagerstroemia fauriei*: in early spring
- *Lagerstroemia indica*: in early spring
- *Lagerstroemia speciosa*: in early spring

WHICH TOOLS

- Hand pruners
- Long-handled pruners (loppers)

FORMATIVE PRUNING

When they are grown as shrubs, young plants should be pruned so they grow bushy and well-structured, with a central main stem and plenty of branches originating from it. This could be converted into a standard with a single stem later on if wished. Remove the top 4–6in (10–15cm) of the main stem to encourage branching along its length. In early spring, cut any weak, leggy shoots back to two or three buds. Remove the end third of any long, straggly shoots.

ROUTINE PRUNING

Once a framework of branches has been established, annual pruning will remove about one-half of the smaller (sublateral) branches to encourage new flower-bearing shoots. In early spring, cut shoots back to within two or three buds of the lateral stems, which form the plant's main framework of branches. Remove any branches that cross through the middle of the plant.

REMEDIAL PRUNING

These plants can be cut back quite severely—even back to the main framework of branches—to promote new growth or to overcome frost damage. Remove all the small branches and cut the framework branches back to within four or five buds of the main stem.

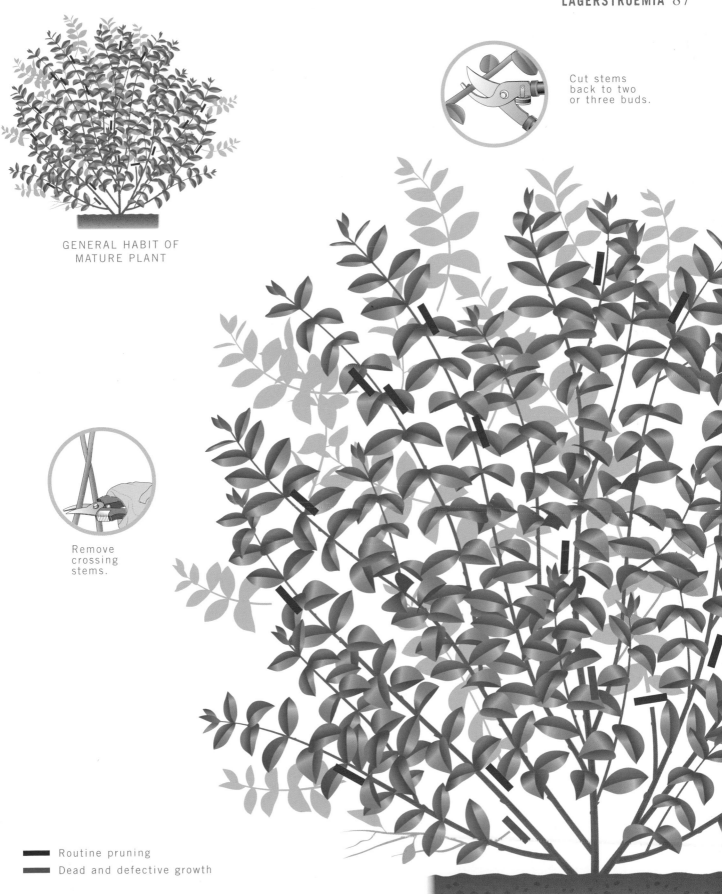

GENERAL HABIT OF
MATURE PLANT

Cut stems
back to two
or three buds.

Remove
crossing
stems.

Routine pruning
Dead and defective growth

LAVANDULA
Lavender

The wonderful scent and beautiful colors of both flowers and foliage have made lavender one of the best known and best loved of all garden plants.

WHY PRUNE?
To promote flowering and to create a compact, bushy plant.

PRUNING TIPS
Trim the dead flowers off *L. stoechas* after flowering but leave the main pruning until spring.

WHEN TO PRUNE MOST SPECIES
Early to midspring or late summer

PLANTS PRUNED THIS WAY
- *Lavandula angustifolia* and cvs.: after flowering
- *Lavandula ×intermedia* and cvs.: after flowering
- *Lavandula stoechas* and cvs.: in spring
- *Hebe pinguifolia* and cvs.: after flowering
- *Hebe speciosa* and cvs.: in spring

WHICH TOOLS
- Hand pruners
- Shears

FORMATIVE PRUNING
Prune young plants to encourage them to develop a bushy habit, with strong shoots emerging from the base of the plant. After planting, cut out any weak or damaged growth. Cut the remaining shoots back to about half of their length to encourage new shoots to form at the base of the plant.

ROUTINE PRUNING
Pruning is necessary not only to remove spent flowers and keep the plants compact and bushy, but also to encourage production of plenty of new shoots to prevent bareness at the base. Remove any broken, damaged, or winter-killed shoots and trim back tall stems in spring. Prune after flowering by removing the dead flowerheads with about 2–3in (5–7cm) of leafy growth.

REMEDIAL PRUNING
These short-lived shrubs often become bare and leggy at the base. They do not respond to severe pruning, and the old wood does not produce new shoots. Remove and replace old, straggly plants.

GENERAL HABIT OF
MATURE PLANT

Remove
dead
flowers.

Remove dead or
damaged stems.

Routine pruning
Dead and defective growth

LONICERA
Climbing honeysuckle

There is nothing to compare with the scent of honeysuckle on a warm summer evening. If there is one fragrant plant that should be grown close to open windows, this is it.

WHY PRUNE?
To control the plant and to encourage production of flower-bearing shoots.

PRUNING TIPS
Use sharp pruners because the stems are easily crushed.

WHEN TO PRUNE MOST SPECIES
Late summer

PLANTS PRUNED THIS WAY
- *Lonicera caprifolium* and cvs.: in late summer, after flowering
- *Lonicera etrusca* and cvs.: in late summer, after flowering
- *Lonicera henryi* and cvs.: in late summer, after flowering
- *Lonicera japonica* and cvs.: in spring, after flowering
- *Lonicera periclymenum* and cvs.: in late summer, after flowering
- *Lonicera sempervirens* (native honeysuckle): in late summer, after flowering

WHICH TOOLS
- Hand pruners
- Long-handled pruners (loppers)

FORMATIVE PRUNING
Prune young plants to encourage them to develop a bushy habit, with strong shoots emerging from the base of the plant. After planting, cut out any weak or damaged growth. Cut the remaining shoots back to about one-third of their length to encourage development of new shoots from the base of the plant as it becomes established. Select the strongest shoots and tie them to the support until they start to twine of their own accord.

ROUTINE PRUNING
Try to produce a framework of strong, healthy shoots and to encourage formation of flower-producing spurs. Mature plants need to be pruned to stay contained within their allotted area. In late summer after flowering, cut back all shoots that are growing beyond their allotted space. Cut back to 2ft (60cm) inside the allotted area to allow the shoots to branch. Thin out congested growth. Cut all lateral shoots back to within two or three buds of the main stems—these will bear next season's flowers.

REMEDIAL PRUNING
Unless they are pruned regularly, climbing honeysuckles become tangled masses of old and new growth. The overcrowding often leads to pests and diseases. In late winter or early spring, cut the plant back to a framework of three or four main branches about 2ft (60cm) long. This will encourage development of new shoots. Six to eight weeks after cutting down the plant, remove all the weak, thin shoots and leave up to six of the strongest, healthiest shoots.

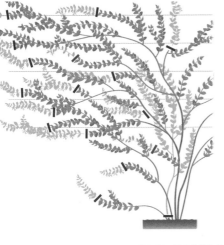

GENERAL HABIT OF
MATURE PLANT

Tie in main
growth.

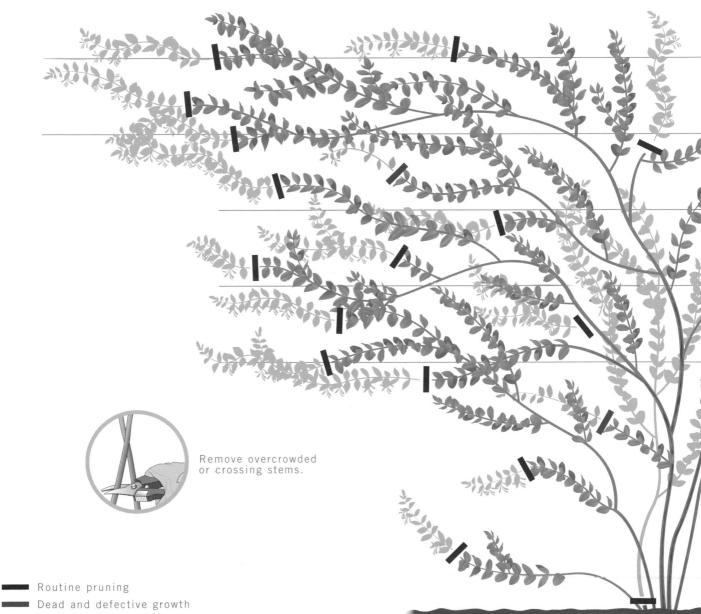

Remove overcrowded
or crossing stems.

Routine pruning
Dead and defective growth

LONICERA
Shrubby honeysuckle, twinberry

Shrubby forms of honeysuckle are invaluable hedging plants, and freestanding specimens make good focal points, especially when they are topiarized.

WHY PRUNE?
To restrict height and to encourage the plant to develop a more open, balanced habit.

PRUNING TIPS
Use a pruning saw to remove older stems, which might be crushed by long-handled pruners (loppers).

WHEN TO PRUNE MOST SPECIES
Late spring or early summer

PLANTS PRUNED THIS WAY
- *Deutzia gracilis* and cvs.: in late spring or early summer
- *Forsythia ×intermedia* and cvs.: in late spring or early summer
- *Lonicera tartarica* and cvs.: in midsummer
- *Lonicera fragrantissima*: in late spring or early summer
- *Lonicera ×purpusii* and cvs.: in late spring or early summer
- *Lonicera standishii*: in late spring or early summer

WHICH TOOLS
- Hand pruners
- Pruning saw

FORMATIVE PRUNING
Prune young plants to encourage them to develop a bushy habit, with strong shoots emerging from close to ground level. After planting, cut out any weak or damaged growth. Lightly pinch off the remaining shoots to about two-thirds of their length so that new shoots grow from the base of the plant.

ROUTINE PRUNING
Shrubby honeysuckles should be pruned regularly if they are to flower well. It is important to remove the old wood, which would gradually accumulate, and to encourage production of new flower-bearing shoots. Immediately after flowering, cut the old flower-bearing stems back to a strong pair of buds or down to lower, younger shoots. Pruning in early summer gives the plant the maximum period of growth for a good display of flowers the following year. Cut old flower-bearing stems back by at least half, cutting to just above a healthy bud or to a well-placed new sideshoot. Remove about one-quarter of the old stems each year to allow new shoots to develop.

REMEDIAL PRUNING
Old shrubs, especially if they have not been pruned regularly, will naturally become overcrowded as they age and develop into a thicket of thin, weak, straggly stems that produce few flowers. This can be remedied with hard pruning. In late winter or early spring, cut the shoots back to a framework of four or five shoots within 18–24in (45–60cm) of ground level to encourage new growth.

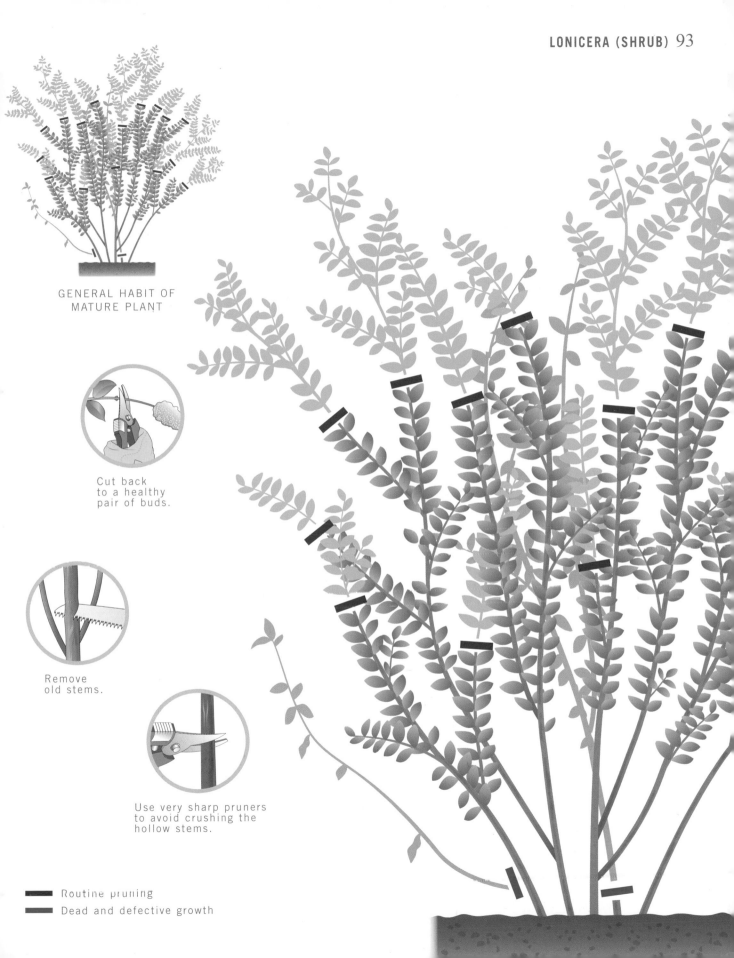

GENERAL HABIT OF
MATURE PLANT

Cut back
to a healthy
pair of buds.

Remove
old stems.

Use very sharp pruners
to avoid crushing the
hollow stems.

—— Routine pruning
—— Dead and defective growth

MAGNOLIA
Magnolia

Magnolia flowers are among the most beautiful of all blooms, and a tree laden with the spectacular flowers is an unforgettable sight.

WHY PRUNE?
To maintain a balanced shape and to encourage flowering.

PRUNING TIPS
Always prune when plants are in full leaf so that the cuts don't bleed excessively.

WHEN TO PRUNE MOST SPECIES
Midsummer

PLANTS PRUNED THIS WAY
- *Magnolia grandiflora* and other evergreen species: in spring
- *Magnolia liliiflora*: in midsummer, while in leaf
- *Magnolia ×soulangeana* and cvs.: in midsummer, while in leaf
- *Magnolia stellata* and cvs.: in midsummer, while in leaf

WHICH TOOLS
- Hand pruners
- Pruning saw

FORMATIVE PRUNING
Young plants require only light pruning to encourage the development of multistemmed plants that are evenly balanced with strong shoots. In spring, remove any weak, damaged, or broken shoots. Cut out any shoots growing across the center of the bush. Pinch back any long, vigorous shoots by removing the end third of each shoot.

ROUTINE PRUNING
Magnolias do not require regular pruning to keep growing well, but vigorous shoots can be cut back to balance the growth and shape of the plant. Cut vigorous stems back at least halfway along their length to just above a healthy bud or to a well-placed sideshoot. Cut back any shoots or branches that have been damaged by wind. Immediately after flowering, deadhead by cutting back the old flower-bearing spikes to a strong, healthy bud or down to a lower, strongly growing shoot.

REMEDIAL PRUNING
As they age, magnolias produce less extension growth at the tip of each shoot and only slowly increase in overall size. Because the wood is brittle, they are often damaged by strong winds, and remedial pruning should be carried out in stages over three or four years. Multistemmed plants can be revived by cutting between one-quarter and one-third of the old stems back to 2–3ft (60cm–1m) above soil level. The following year, repeat the process, and thin out any overcrowded new shoots to allow the stronger stems to grow. Repeat this process over several years until all the old wood has been replaced.

GENERAL HABIT OF
MATURE PLANT

Remove dead
flowers and
cut back to a
healthy bud.

Cut vigorous
shoots back to
a healthy bud.

Remove dead or
damaged stems.

■ Routine pruning
▬ Dead and defective growth

MAHONIA
Mahonia

There can be few sights more heartening in winter than the golden-yellow flowers of mahonia. As if this was not enough, the flowers carry their heady lily-of-the-valley fragrance on the winter breezes.

WHY PRUNE?

To restrict the plant's height and to encourage it to develop a bushy habit of growth.

PRUNING TIPS

- Start pruning before the new shoots form to avoid losing next year's flowers.
- Use bypass pruners because anvil-type pruners will easily crush the stems.
- Wear thick leather gloves to protect yourself from the spiny leaves.

WHEN TO PRUNE MOST SPECIES

Early or midspring

PLANTS PRUNED THIS WAY

- *Mahonia aquifolium* and cvs.: in spring, after flowering
- *Mahonia fortunei* and cvs.: in spring, after flowering
- *Mahonia repens* and cvs.: in spring, after flowering
- *Mahonia* ×*media* and cvs.: in spring, after flowering
- *Nandina domestica* and cvs.: in midsummer, after flowering

WHICH TOOLS

- Bypass pruners
- Long-handled pruners (loppers)
- Thornproof leather gloves

FORMATIVE PRUNING

Try to encourage the development of a multistemmed plant with strong shoots forming close to ground level. In the first spring after planting, cut back the woody stems to the lowest whorl or cluster of leaves, preferably to 6–8in (15–20cm) above ground level.

ROUTINE PRUNING

Although no regular pruning is required, its goal would be to form a multibranched plant and to prevent it from becoming too tall, straggly, and unmanageable. In spring, after the flowers have faded, cut back stems to the desired height. This will allow the maximum period of growth to produce a good display of flowers the following year, but it will also sacrifice the current year's berries. Cut the stems at a point just above a whorl of leaves to encourage the dormant buds to produce between three and five new stems from this point. Cut out any thin, straggling growths because they rarely produce good flowers and often harbor pests and diseases.

REMEDIAL PRUNING

As it ages—especially if it has been neglected for a number of years—mahonia tends to shed its lower leaves, often leaving the base of each stem bare and leggy and exposing old bark, which is marked with deep cracks and fissures. Plants will, however, usually respond to hard pruning. Cut the plant back to a framework of strong shoots within 1–2ft (30–60cm) above ground level in late spring. Pruning too early in the year leaves the new shoots at risk from spring frosts. Prune any thin or weak shoots back to stronger stems or to ground level.

GENERAL HABIT OF
MATURE PLANT

Remove thin,
weak growth.

Remedial pruning: Cut back
to within 1–2ft (30–60cm)
of ground level.

Routine pruning
Dead and defective growth

MALUS
Crab apple

These ornamental relatives of the fruiting apple (*Malus domestica*) are among the most widely grown of spring-flowering trees. The glorious display of blossom is often accompanied by attractive young foliage in shades of lime green, bronze, or red-purple.

WHY PRUNE?

To produce and maintain new, healthy growth and to improve flowering.

PRUNING TIPS

Don't prune too severely, or the plant will produce water shoots and suckers.

WHEN TO PRUNE MOST SPECIES

Mid- or late summer

PLANTS PRUNED THIS WAY

- *Malus baccata* and cvs.: in mid- or late summer, or after flowering
- *Malus floribunda* and cvs.: in mid- or late summer, or after flowering
- *Pyrus calleryana* and cvs.: in mid- or late summer, or after flowering

WHICH TOOLS

- Hand pruners
- Long-handled pruners (loppers)
- Pruning saw

FORMATIVE PRUNING

Crab apples are usually trained as standard trees with a main, single stem, but the branch structure or head (crown) of the tree can be developed after the plant has started to grow in your garden. Prune young plants to encourage the development of a well-balanced head with a central stem and laterals coming from it. After planting, cut out any damaged growth. Cut the remaining shoots back to about half of their length, leaving the main stem in the head slightly longer than those around it. Cut back any small, lateral shoots to 3–4in (7–10cm) to encourage the development of new shoots.

ROUTINE PRUNING

Once the branch structure has developed—which will take about five years—little routine pruning is needed, although you should remove any damaged growth. Any pruning is best done in summer as soon as possible after flowering, when it will not encourage excessively vigorous growth and will minimize the chances of fungal attack. Cut back any shoots that are rubbing or split. Remove any competing or overcrowded branches. Remove suckers originating below the graft.

REMEDIAL PRUNING

Crab apples often become thick and congested with age, with thin, weak, straggly branches. They then produce fewer flowers, especially if pruning has been neglected. This can be overcome by removing weak or diseased growth, opening up the tree in the center for good air circulation.

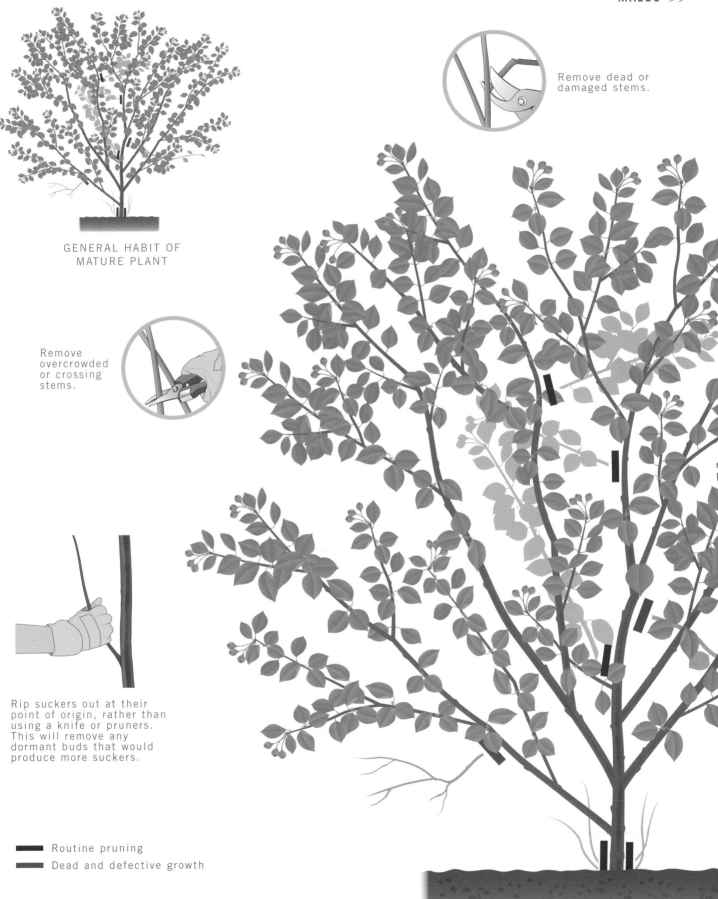

GENERAL HABIT OF
MATURE PLANT

Remove dead or
damaged stems.

Remove
overcrowded
or crossing
stems.

Rip suckers out at their
point of origin, rather than
using a knife or pruners.
This will remove any
dormant buds that would
produce more suckers.

Routine pruning
Dead and defective growth

OSMANTHUS
Sweet olive, devil wood

These compact, easy-to-grow shrubs or small trees produce small but wonderfully fragrant flowers, which are followed by attractive berries.

WHY PRUNE?

To encourage flowers and to encourage the plant to develop a bushy, well-balanced habit.

PRUNING TIPS

Osmanthus species can be sheared in summer where they are used as hedge plants or topiaries, but this removes many of the following year's flower buds.

WHEN TO PRUNE MOST SPECIES

Late spring

PLANTS PRUNED THIS WAY

- *Osmanthus armatus* and cvs. (bloom in late summer or fall): in early spring
- *Osmanthus delavayi* and cvs.: in late spring, after flowering
- *Osmanthus fragrans*: in early spring
- *Osmanthus heterophyllus* and cvs. (bloom in late summer or fall): in early spring
- *Osmanthus ×burkwoodii* and cvs.: in late spring, after flowering

WHICH TOOLS

- Hand pruners
- Long-handled pruners (loppers)
- Pruning saw

FORMATIVE PRUNING

Light pruning will encourage development of a multistemmed shrub, with strong shoots forming an evenly balanced plant. In spring, remove any damaged or broken shoots. Cut back any shoots growing across the center of the bush. Prune the remaining shoots by removing about one-third of each shoot. Cut back vigorous shoots by about half to keep the growth even and balanced.

ROUTINE PRUNING

These plants do not require regular pruning to keep growing well, but vigorous shoots should be cut back to balance the growth and shape of the plant. Cut vigorous stems back by at least half their length to just above a healthy bud or to a well-placed sideshoot. Remove any thin, weak growth from the center of the plant. Remove any new growth that has been damaged by late frosts.

REMEDIAL PRUNING

As they age, these shrubs produce less extension growth at the tip of each shoot and increase in overall size only slowly. At the same time, they often become bare and straggly at the base, and sometimes the branches splay out, leaving an open center. Cut back all stems to 18–24in (45–60cm) above ground level in late spring. In summer, remove any thin, overcrowded shoots to allow the stronger stems to grow.

GENERAL HABIT OF
MATURE PLANT

Cut vigorous
stems back to
a healthy bud.

Remove frost-
damaged growth.

Remove thin,
weak growth.

▬ Routine pruning
═ Dead and defective growth

PASSIFLORA
Granadilla, passionflower

The spectacular flowers alone make these plants worth growing, but they have the added advantage of producing edible yellow fruits in late summer and fall.

WHY PRUNE?
To control the plant and to encourage flowers.

PRUNING TIPS
Avoid hard pruning, which may reduce flowering for the next year or two.

WHEN TO PRUNE MOST SPECIES
Early spring

PLANTS PRUNED THIS WAY
- *Lonicera etrusca*: in spring
- *Lonicera japonica*: in spring
- *Lonicera periclymenum*: in late summer, after flowering
- *Passiflora caerulea*: in spring

WHICH TOOLS
- Hand pruners
- Long-handled pruners (loppers)

FORMATIVE PRUNING

Prune young plants to encourage them to develop a bushy habit, with strong shoots emerging from the base of the plant or to climb a supporting structure. After planting, cut out any weak or damaged growth. Cut the remaining shoots back to about one-third of their length to encourage new shoots to grow from the base of the plant. Select the strongest four or five shoots and tie them to the trellis or wires until they form tendrils and start to take hold of the support.

ROUTINE PRUNING

Try to produce a framework of strong, healthy shoots and form flower-producing spurs. Mature plants are pruned to stay contained within their allotted area. In spring, cut out any weak, dead, or frost-damaged shoots. Thin out congested growth and cut all lateral shoots back to within two or three buds of the main stems—these will bear the new season's flowers.

REMEDIAL PRUNING

Even when they are pruned regularly, passionflowers become a tangled mass of old and new growth, and the overcrowding often leads to pests and diseases. Remove old, straggly plants and replace them with a new specimen.

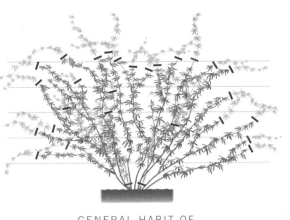

GENERAL HABIT OF
MATURE PLANT

Remove tendrils before
pruning stems to ease
removal of the stems
from the support.

Tie in main
growth.

Remove
overcrowded
or crossing
stems.

▬▬ Routine pruning
▬▬ Dead and defective growth

PHILADELPHUS

Mock orange

If there is one shrub you should get when you start gardening, it is a mock orange. In early to midsummer, it will be covered with cascades of small, fragrant flowers, carried along the arching branches.

FORMATIVE PRUNING

Prune young plants to encourage them to develop into bushy shrubs with strong shoots emerging from soil level. After planting, cut out any damaged growth. Cut the remaining shoots back to about half of their length to encourage new shoots to develop from the base of the plant.

ROUTINE PRUNING

If they are to flower well, mock oranges need regular annual pruning to remove the old wood that would gradually accumulate, and to encourage the production of new flower-bearing shoots. Try to remove about one-quarter of the old stems each year to allow in light and make room for new shoots to develop. Cut back the old wood as close to the ground as possible in late summer to allow the maximum period of growth to produce a good display of flowers the following year. Shape the plant by cutting old flower-bearing stems back to just above a healthy bud or to a well-placed new sideshoot.

REMEDIAL PRUNING

Mock oranges often become thick and overcrowded as they age, with thin, weak, straggly stems and fewer flowers, especially if pruning has been neglected. This can be overcome with hard pruning in stages over several years. Select three or four strong stems and cut them back to about half of their length. Cut the remaining shoots back to within 2–3in (5–7cm) of ground level to encourage new shoots to develop to replace the old ones. The following year, completely remove any thin or weak shoots. Cut out the three or four remaining old stems close to ground level.

WHY PRUNE?

To encourage the plant to develop new flower-bearing shoots.

PRUNING TIPS

Use bypass hand pruners because the stems are easily crushed by anvil-type hand pruners.

WHEN TO PRUNE MOST SPECIES

Late summer

PLANTS PRUNED THIS WAY

- *Philadelphus coronarius* and cvs.: in late summer, after flowering
- *Philadelphus* 'Manteau d'Hermine' and all other named cvs.: in late summer, after flowering
- *Kerria japonica* and cvs.: in late spring, after flowering

WHICH TOOLS

- Hand pruners
- Long-handled pruners (loppers)
- Pruning saw

GENERAL HABIT OF
MATURE PLANT

Cut old flower-
bearing stems back
to a healthy bud.

Remove
old stems.

▬ Routine pruning
▬ Dead and defective growth

POTENTILLA FRUTICOSA

Cinquefoil, shrubby cinquefoil

These tolerant, easy-to-grow shrubs are covered with colorful flowers, and it is possible to choose forms that will provide flowers from summer through late fall.

FORMATIVE PRUNING

Prune young plants to encourage a bushy habit, with strong shoots emerging from the base of the plant. After planting, cut out any weak or damaged growth. Cut the remaining shoots back to about half their length to promote new shoots at the base of the plant.

ROUTINE PRUNING

It is important to remove the spent flowers and to keep the plants compact and bushy. Pruning should encourage plants to produce lots of new shoots so that they do not become bare at the base. In midspring, trim back any long, vigorous shoots. Cut about one-third of the oldest stems back to ground level and cut out any congested growth. After flowering, prune the dead flowerheads along with 2–3in (5–7cm) of leafy growth.

REMEDIAL PRUNING

Potentillas become woody and overcrowded as they age, with lots of thin, weak, straggly stems producing fewer and smaller flowers. This can be overcome with hard pruning, but the flowers will be lost for the following season. In late winter or early spring, cut the old, strong shoots back to within 4–6in (10–15cm) of ground level, and cut out any thin, weak growth to develop new shoots.

WHY PRUNE?
To promote flowering and to create a compact, bushy plant.

PRUNING TIPS
Use shears to trim the plants after flowering.

WHEN TO PRUNE MOST SPECIES
Midspring

PLANTS PRUNED THIS WAY
- *Cistus* spp. and cvs.: in midspring
- *Hebe albicans*: in spring and after flowering
- *Hebe rakaiensis*: in spring and after flowering
- *Potentilla fruticosa* and cvs.: in midspring

WHICH TOOLS
- Hand pruners
- Pruning shears

GENERAL HABIT OF
MATURE PLANT

Remove
dead
flowers.

Remove
overvigorous
stems.

Remove
old stems.

Routine pruning

Dead and defective growth

PRUNUS
(deciduous species)

Flowering cherry, ornamental cherry

Flowering cherries provide glorious displays of blossoms, often on bare stems in early to midspring and often leaving a dense carpet of fallen petals at the base of the plant when flowering is finally over.

WHY PRUNE?

To maintain a balanced framework of branches.

PRUNING TIPS

Prune after flowering, to reduce the risk of fungal diseases.

WHEN TO PRUNE MOST SPECIES

Late spring

PLANTS PRUNED THIS WAY

• *Prunus subhirtella* and cvs.: in late spring, after flowering (if necessary)

WHICH TOOLS

• Hand pruners
• Pruning saw

FORMATIVE PRUNING

Prune young plants to encourage them to grow bushy and well structured, with a main central stem and plenty of well-spaced branches originating from it. Remove the top 4–6in (10–15cm) of the main stem to encourage branching along its length. In summer, cut out any weak, leggy shoots. Remove the end third of any long, straggly shoots.

ROUTINE PRUNING

Most flowering cherries will grow well for many years with little or no pruning, and on the whole they should not be pruned unless they have congested, diseased, or damaged growth. Cut out sucker growth that originates below the graft and any crossing or damaged branches by pruning them back to their point of origin.

REMEDIAL PRUNING

These plants do not respond well to severe pruning, and the best course is to replace an old, poorly flowering specimen with a new plant. Remove and dispose of old, misshapen plants.

GENERAL HABIT OF
MATURE PLANT

Remove
overcrowded
or crossing
branches.

Remove dead or
damaged growth.

Routine pruning
Dead and defective growth

PRUNUS
(evergreen species)
Cherry laurel, Portugal laurel

The evergreen forms of Prunus are not usually grown for their flowers but often to help give a garden a framework. They are some of the best evergreen plants for use as hedges, freestanding shrubs, or groundcover.

FORMATIVE PRUNING

Prune young plants to encourage them to grow bushy, with strong shoots emerging from within 12in (30cm) of soil level. After planting, cut out any weak or damaged growth. Cut the remaining shoots back by about one-third to encourage development of new shoots from the base of the plant as it becomes established.

ROUTINE PRUNING

Pruning is done in the late winter after the brightly colored berries are gone and after the risk of severe frost has passed or after flowering. Try to maintain a well-balanced shape and encourage healthy, glossy foliage. Cut back any excessively vigorous shoots to help the plant retain its natural shape. On variegated plants, remove any all-green shoots. Prune back to a strong bud all the old flower- and fruit-bearing spikes from the previous year.

REMEDIAL PRUNING

These shrubs often produce long, bare shoots with only a few leaves on the ends. They also often become bare at the base, revealing dull green stems. Cut down the oldest stems to within 6–8in (15–20cm) of soil level. Cut down to ground level any thin, weak shoots.

WHY PRUNE?

To keep a well-balanced and rounded shape and to prevent plants from becoming bare and straggly at the base.

PRUNING TIPS

Keep pruning to a minimum by choosing a cultivar that will grow to the desired size.

WHEN TO PRUNE MOST SPECIES

Late winter

PLANTS PRUNED THIS WAY

- *Prunus ilicifolia* and cvs.: in late winter, after the berries have gone
- *Prunus laurocerasus* and cvs.: in late winter, after the berries have gone
- *Prunus lusitanica* and cvs.: in late spring or early summer

WHICH TOOLS

- Hand pruners
- Long-handled pruners (loppers)

GENERAL HABIT OF
MATURE PLANT

Cut back to a
healthy bud.

Remove
overvigorous
stems.

Routine pruning
Dead and defective growth

PYRACANTHA

Firethorn

This is one of the best plants you can choose to train against a wall or other flat surface. Once established, it will produce a regular display of brightly colored berries, which often last well into the following spring.

WHY PRUNE?

To produce healthy growth and to keep the plant in its allotted space.

PRUNING TIPS

- Avoid severe pruning, which can lead to fireblight disease (symptoms include the death of new shoots and scorched-looking flowers and leaves).
- Wear strong gloves because the stems are armed with sharp spines.

WHEN TO PRUNE MOST SPECIES

Late spring and late summer

PLANTS PRUNED THIS WAY

- *Pyracantha coccinea*: in late spring, after flowering, and late summer
- *Pyracantha gibbsii*: in late spring, after flowering, and late summer
- *Pyracantha koidzumii*: in late spring, after flowering, and late summer
- *Colletia hystrix*: in midspring
- *Colletia paradoxa*: in midspring

WHICH TOOLS

- Hand pruners
- Long-handled pruners (loppers)
- Thornproof gloves

FORMATIVE PRUNING

Prune young plants to encourage them to grow bushy, with strong shoots emerging from just above soil level that can be trained onto a supporting structure. In the first spring after planting, cut out any weak or damaged growth. Prune the tips of the main shoots by removing the end third of each shoot.

ROUTINE PRUNING

Try to produce a framework of strong, healthy shoots and encourage more shoots. Prune mature plants to keep them within their allotted space. Late-summer pruning will show off the bright berries. To keep the plant tight against the wall, cut back outward-growing shoots to about 4in (10cm) in spring. Remove all old fruit-bearing trusses. In late summer, cut overly vigorous shoots back to two or three buds if they are not required to tie in as part of the framework.

REMEDIAL PRUNING

Pyracanthas often become leggy and bare at the base, but they will respond well to severe pruning. In late winter or early spring, use long-handled pruners (loppers) or a saw to cut all the stems back to within 12in (30cm) of ground level. This will encourage development of new shoots. Six to eight weeks after cutting down the plant, remove all the weak, thin shoots and start to train the new replacement shoots into position on the support structure.

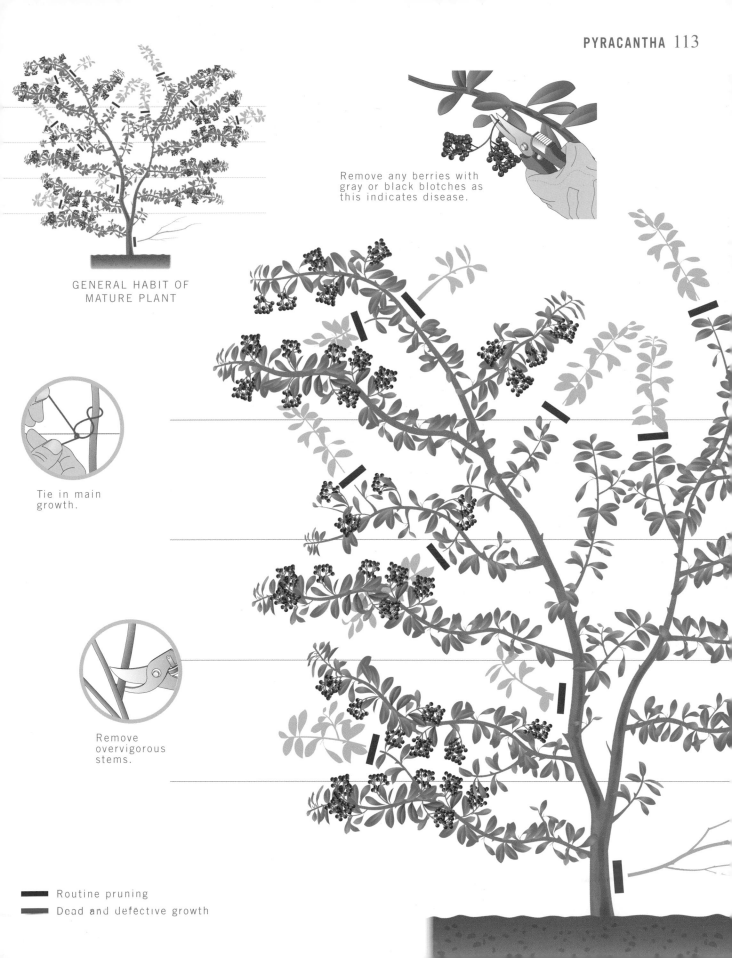

GENERAL HABIT OF
MATURE PLANT

Remove any berries with
gray or black blotches as
this indicates disease.

Tie in main
growth.

Remove
overvigorous
stems.

███ Routine pruning
███ Dead and defective growth

RHODODENDRON

Rhododendron, azalea

These lovely plants range from small specimens, which can be grown in containers, to large shrubs suitable for woodland gardens.

WHY PRUNE?

To encourage flower production and to encourage the plant to develop a bushy habit of growth.

PRUNING TIPS

Start pruning immediately after flowering to avoid losing next year's flowers.

WHEN TO PRUNE MOST SPECIES

Midsummer

PLANTS PRUNED THIS WAY

- *Azalea (Rhododendron* spp. and cvs.) deciduous and evergreen cvs.: in midsummer, after flowering
- *Rhododendron carolinianum* and cvs.: in midsummer, after flowering
- *Rhododendron catawbiense* and cvs.: in midsummer, after flowering
- *Rhododendron maximum* and cvs.: in midsummer, after flowering

WHICH TOOLS

- Hand pruners
- Long-handled pruners (loppers)
- Pruning saw

FORMATIVE PRUNING

Try to encourage the development of a multistemmed plant with strong shoots forming close to ground level. In the first spring after planting, prune the shoots lightly to remove the end third of each shoot. This will form stocky, bushy plants. Cut back vigorous shoots by about half to keep the plant's growth even and balanced.

ROUTINE PRUNING

These plants don't require regular pruning to keep them growing well, but they will do better if dead flowers are removed to prevent the formation of seedheads, which can suppress flowering in subsequent years. Vigorous shoots can be pruned back to keep the growth and shape of the plant balanced. In midsummer, immediately after flowering, cut off the old flower-bearing spikes (deadheading) to a strong, healthy bud or down to lower, stronger shoots. Cut off (and burn) any flower buds that have not opened but that have turned moldy, as these will only spread fungal disease to other parts of the plant. Cut back vigorous stems at least halfway along their length to just above a healthy bud or to a well-placed sideshoot. Remove any thin, weak growths from the center of the plant, and any deadwood. Remove any obvious suckers from the base of the plant by removing them from their below-ground point of origin.

REMEDIAL PRUNING

As they age, rhododendrons produce less extension growth at the tip of each shoot and increase in overall size slowly. They often become bare and straggly at the base. Cut back just the older stems to 12–18in (30–45cm) above soil level in spring. In late summer, remove any thin or overcrowded shoots to allow the stronger stems to grow.

GENERAL HABIT OF
MATURE PLANT

Cut old flower-
bearing stems back
to a heatlhy bud.

Cut vigorous
stems back to
a healthy bud.

Remedial pruning:
Cut back old stems.

Routine pruning
Dead and defective growth

ROSA
Large-flowered roses

These popular plants, known for their colorful and often fragrant flowers, are possibly the most widely grown of all hardy plants. There can be few gardens without at least one rosebush in them.

WHY PRUNE?
To encourage the production of strong, new shoots and flushes of blooms.

PRUNING TIPS
Don't prune when a frost is forecast, because the pruned stems may split, especially if the sap is flowing.

WHEN TO PRUNE MOST SPECIES
Late winter or early spring

PLANTS PRUNED THIS WAY
- *Rosa* 'Fragrant Cloud': in late winter or early spring
- *Rosa* 'Piccadilly': in late winter or early spring
- *Rosa* 'Ruby Wedding': in late winter or early spring
- *Rosa* 'Silver Jubilee': in late winter or early spring

WHICH TOOLS
- Hand pruners
- Long-handled pruners (loppers)
- Pruning saw

FORMATIVE PRUNING
Try to encourage the development of a multistemmed plant with strong shoots forming close to ground level to create a balanced framework of branches. Remove damaged or broken shoots and cut back any shoots growing across the center of the bush. Prune back strong, healthy shoots to within 3–6in (7–15cm) of ground level, cutting to an outward-facing bud.

ROUTINE PRUNING
This type of rose needs regular annual pruning to produce an open-centered plant with good air circulation. In late winter or early spring, cut back any dead, diseased, or damaged stems as close to the healthy branches as possible. Always try to cut back to an outward-facing bud so that the center of the bush does not become congested. Remove thin, weak shoots or shoots growing across the center of the bush. If the old growth stubs have become overcrowded, remove them with a small pruning saw. Cut back any shoots that are crossing close to one another, because stems that rub against each other will damage the bark and leave the rose open to disease. Finally, cut back all remaining shoots to about 10in (25cm) above soil level, cutting just above an outward-facing bud. Thinner shoots can be cut back to 6in (15cm).

REMEDIAL PRUNING
Roses that are left unpruned tend to become overcrowded, producing poor flowers and leaving the plant susceptible to pests and diseases. This can be overcome by hard pruning, done in stages to minimize the likelihood of suckers emerging from the rootstock. In winter, cut back half of the old stems as close to the old branch framework as possible, using a saw if necessary. Leave stubs, 1–2in (2.5–5cm) long, from which the new shoots will emerge. In the second year, completely cut out any thin or weak shoots and remove any old branches that still remain.

GENERAL HABIT OF
MATURE PLANT

Remove
dead or
damaged
stems.

Remove overcrowded
or crossing stems.

FORMATIVE PRUNING

First spring

▬▬ Routine pruning
▭▭ Dead and defective growth

ROSA

Cluster-flowered roses

These popular plants have colorful—often fragrant—flowers and are most commonly grown for a mass display of color rather than for the individual blooms.

WHY PRUNE?

To encourage the production of strong new shoots and flushes of blooms.

PRUNING TIPS

Don't prune when a frost is forecast, because the pruned stems may split, especially if the sap is flowing.

WHEN TO PRUNE MOST SPECIES

Late winter or early spring

PLANTS PRUNED THIS WAY

- *Rosa* 'Anne Harkness': in late winter or early spring, before new growth begins
- *Rosa* 'Iceberg': in late winter or early spring, before new growth begins
- *Rosa* 'Margaret Merril': in late winter or early spring, before new growth begins
- *Rosa* 'Queen Elizabeth': in late winter or early spring, before new growth begins

WHICH TOOLS

- Hand pruners
- Pruning saw
- Thornproof leather gloves

FORMATIVE PRUNING

Try to encourage the development of a multistemmed plant with strong shoots forming close to ground level to create a balanced framework of branches. Remove damaged or broken shoots and cut back any shoots growing across the center of the bush. Prune back all strong, healthy shoots to within 3–6in (7–15cm) of ground level, cutting to an outward-facing bud.

ROUTINE PRUNING

These roses need regular annual pruning to produce an open-centered plant with good air circulation. In late winter or early spring, cut back dead, diseased, or damaged stems as close to healthy branches as possible. Always try to cut back to an outward-facing bud so that the center of the bush does not become congested. Remove any thin, weak shoots or shoots growing across the center of the bush. If the old stubs of growth have become overcrowded, remove them with a small pruning saw. Cut back any shoots that are crossing or rubbing together and causing damage. Finally, cut back all remaining shoots to about 4in (10cm) above where the previous year's growth started. After about four years of this treatment, cut these stems to about 10in (25cm) above soil level. Also remove thinner shoots.

REMEDIAL PRUNING

Roses left unpruned tend to become overcrowded, producing poor flowers and leaving the plant susceptible to pests and diseases. This can be overcome by hard pruning, done in stages to minimize the likelihood of suckers emerging from the rootstock. In winter, prune half of the old stems as close to the old branch framework as possible, using a saw if necessary. Leave stubs, 1–2in (2.5–5cm) long, from which the new shoots will emerge. In the second year, cut out any weak shoots and any remaining old branches. Cut the strong stems back to 10in (25cm) above soil level.

GENERAL HABIT OF
MATURE PLANT

Remove thin,
weak growth.

Remove dead or
damaged stems.

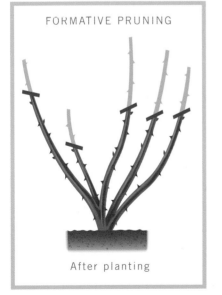

FORMATIVE PRUNING

After planting

━━ Routine pruning
━━ Dead and defective growth

ROSA

Shrub and species roses

Many of the roses in this group are included in gardens for their colorful—sometimes fragrant—flowers. They can be grown for a mass display of color or as individual plants, and some will also produce attractive fruits, known as hips.

WHY PRUNE?

To encourage the production of strong new shoots, flushes of blooms, and colorful hips.

PRUNING TIPS

Check regularly for suckers, which may look similar to the cultivated roses but emerge from below the graft, and remove them as soon as you can.

WHEN TO PRUNE MOST SPECIES

Late winter or early spring

PLANTS PRUNED THIS WAY

- *Rosa xanthina* 'Canary Bird': in late winter or early spring, before new growth begins
- *Rosa glauca*: in late winter or early spring, before new growth begins
- *Rosa moyesii*: in late winter or early spring, before new growth begins
- *Rosa gallica* 'Versicolor': in late winter or early spring, before new growth begins
- *Rosa chinensis* 'Viridiflora': in late winter or early spring, before new growth begins

WHICH TOOLS

- Hand pruners
- Long-handled pruners (loppers)
- Thornproof leather gloves

FORMATIVE PRUNING

Try to encourage the development of a multistemmed plant with strong shoots forming close to ground level to create a balanced framework of branches. Remove damaged or broken shoots and cut back any shoots growing across the center of the bush. Prune back the strong, healthy shoots to within 3–6in (7–15cm) of ground level, cutting to an outward-facing bud.

ROUTINE PRUNING

These roses need regular annual pruning to produce an open-centered plant that allows good air circulation, to remove any old and diseased wood, and to encourage the production of vigorous new shoots. In late winter or early spring, cut back any dead, diseased, or damaged stems as close to the healthy branches as possible. You can prune healthy stems of modern shrub roses by one-third to a half. Always try to cut back to an outward-facing bud so that the center of the bush does not become congested. Completely remove one or two old, woody stems close to the base. Cut out thin, weak shoots or shoots growing across the center of the bush. If the old stubs of growth have become overcrowded, remove them with a small pruning saw. After flowering, remove the end third of each flowering shoot (unless the plants are being grown for their colorful hips).

REMEDIAL PRUNING

Shrub and species roses naturally become overcrowded because they produce a dense mass of thin, weak, straggly stems, which are often susceptible to pests and diseases. This can be overcome by hard pruning, which is better done in stages. In late winter, cut back half the old stems as close to ground level as possible. Reduce the remaining shoots to about half their original length. In the following summer, completely cut out any thin or weak shoots and remove any old branches.

GENERAL HABIT OF
MATURE PLANT

Remove thin,
weak growth.

FORMATIVE PRUNING

After planting

Remove
old stems.

— Routine pruning
— Dead and defective growth

ROSA
Climbers

In high summer, a wall or pergola covered with a climbing rose in full bloom is an unforgettable sight, with the beautiful flowers nestling among the vivid green leaves.

WHY PRUNE?
To encourage the production of strong, new shoots and flushes of blooms.

PRUNING TIPS
Tie as many shoots as possible into a horizontal position.

WHEN TO PRUNE MOST SPECIES
Early or mid-fall

PLANTS PRUNED THIS WAY
- *Rosa* 'Altissimo': in fall
- *Rosa* 'Handel': in fall
- *Rosa* 'New Dawn': in fall
- *Rosa* 'Zepherine Drouhin': in fall

WHICH TOOLS
- Hand pruners
- Long-handled pruners (loppers)
- Pruning knife

FORMATIVE PRUNING

Try to encourage the development of a multistemmed plant with strong shoots forming close to ground level and to create a balanced framework of branches. Remove damaged or broken shoots. Cut back any shoots that are growing across the center of the plant. As they develop, prune back the tips of strong, healthy shoots when they reach 30–36in (75–90cm) high by removing the last 4in (10cm) of each shoot to encourage branching.

ROUTINE PRUNING

Regular pruning should remove old, dead, and diseased wood and any weak, thin shoots and encourage vigorous new shoots. This will create short, flower-bearing spurs, which can be encouraged by training shoots horizontally. In fall, cut back any dead, diseased, or damaged stems as close to ground level as possible. Each year, try to remove about one-third of the oldest flower-bearing stems to make room for the new shoots. After flowering has finished, cut back any flower-bearing lateral shoots by two-thirds of their total length. Cut back any shoots that are crossing close to one another and tie in the remaining shoots.

REMEDIAL PRUNING

Left unpruned, many climbing roses will live for many years. They may become bare at the base, but the production of new shoots will gradually stop, and smaller, poorer flowers will result as the plant slowly declines. This can be overcome by hard pruning, which is better done in stages to minimize the chance of suckers emerging from the rootstock. In winter, cut back all the old stems to about two-thirds of their original length to a healthy bud or shoot. Prune the lateral shoots to one-third of their original length. This pruning should encourage new shoots to grow. In the second year, completely cut out any thin or weak shoots. At the same time, remove any old branches that have died.

GENERAL HABIT OF
MATURE PLANT

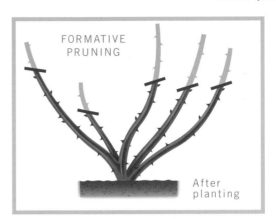

FORMATIVE
PRUNING

After
planting

Tie in new
growth.

Remove thin,
weak growth.

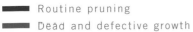

Routine pruning

Dead and defective growth

ROSA

Ramblers

A rambling rose that has been allowed to climb through a tree or trained over a sturdy arch or pergola is a spectacular summer sight.

WHY PRUNE?

To encourage the production of strong new shoots and flushes of blooms.

PRUNING TIPS

Tie in any new growths immediately after pruning so that they are not damaged by strong winds.

WHEN TO PRUNE MOST SPECIES

Early or mid-fall

PLANTS PRUNED THIS WAY

- *Rosa* 'Albertine': after flowering or in early fall
- *Rosa* 'Emily Gray': after flowering or in early fall
- *Rosa* 'New Dawn': after flowering or in early fall
- *Rosa* 'Rambling Rector': after flowering or in early fall
- *Rosa* 'Wedding Day': after flowering or in early fall

WHICH TOOLS

- Hand pruners
- Pruning saw
- Pruning knife
- Thornproof leather gloves

FORMATIVE PRUNING

Try to encourage the development of a multistemmed plant with strong shoots forming close to ground level and to create a balanced framework of branches. Remove any damaged or broken shoots. Cut back any shoots growing across the center of the plant. Prune back the strong, healthy shoots to within 12–16in (30–40cm) of ground level, cutting to an outward-facing bud.

ROUTINE PRUNING

Regular pruning should remove the old, flower-bearing, dead, and diseased wood; cut out weak, thin shoots; encourage vigorous new shoots; and help create short, flower-bearing spurs. Pruning will also keep the plant within its allotted space in the garden. In fall, cut back any dead, diseased, or damaged stems as close to ground level as possible. Each year, try to remove about one-third of the oldest flower-bearing stems to make room for the new shoots. Cut back any shoots that are crossing close or rubbing together and causing damage. Tie in the remaining shoots to the support. After flowering has finished, cut back any flower-bearing lateral shoots to a point about 4in (10cm) from the base of the shoots.

REMEDIAL PRUNING

Old, neglected ramblers tend to become a dense, tangled mass of thin, weak, straggly stems, leaving the plant susceptible to pests and diseases as well as producing only a few poor flowers. This can be overcome by hard pruning, which can be done in stages. Alternatively, the whole plant can be cut down to ground level in late summer. In winter, cut back all old stems to about 18in (45cm) above ground level. This should encourage new shoots to grow. In early summer, cut out any dead and diseased shoots, and remove any thin, weak stems. Tie in the strongest shoots to form the main framework. Prune any lateral shoots to within 4in (10cm) of the main stem or branch.

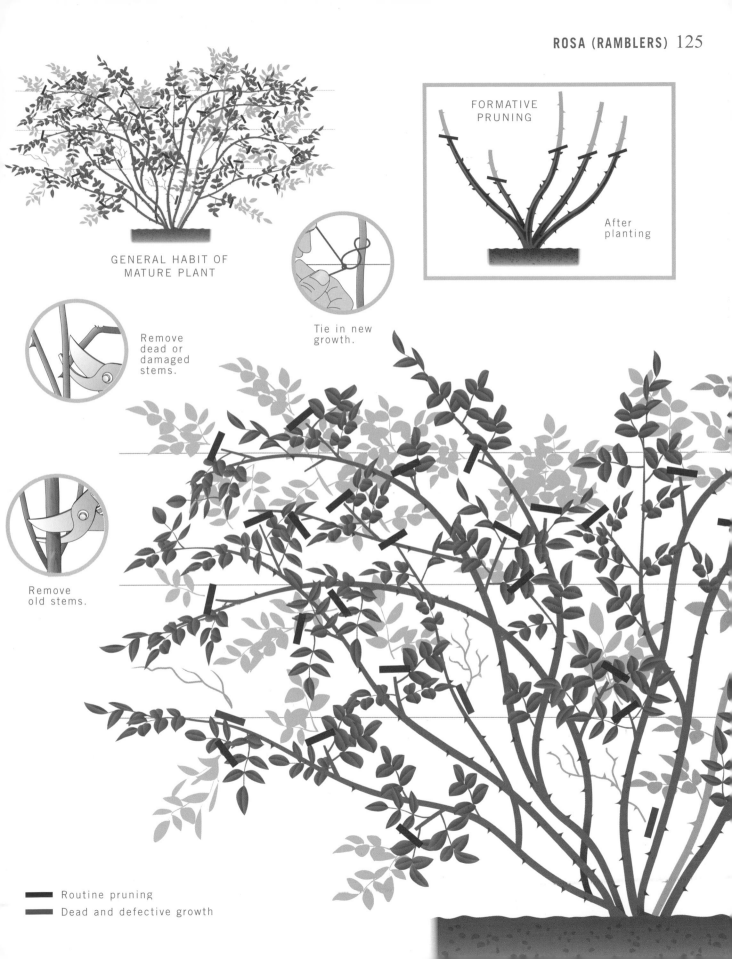

GENERAL HABIT OF
MATURE PLANT

FORMATIVE
PRUNING

After
planting

Tie in new
growth.

Remove
dead or
damaged
stems.

Remove
old stems.

Routine pruning
Dead and defective growth

ROSMARINUS
Rosemary

Valued in the kitchen for its aromatic leaves, rosemary is equally useful in the garden for its structure and vibrant flower color.

WHY PRUNE?
To promote balanced growth.

PRUNING TIPS
To avoid crushing the stems, use a pruning saw for remedial pruning.

WHEN TO PRUNE MOST SPECIES
Late summer

PLANTS PRUNED THIS WAY
- *Rosmarinus officinalis* and cvs.: in late summer, after flowering
- *Santolina* spp. and cvs.: in late summer, after flowering

WHICH TOOLS
- Hand pruners
- Pruning shears

FORMATIVE PRUNING
On the whole, plants should be allowed to develop naturally. Pruning may be necessary to prevent them from becoming unbalanced. After planting, remove any weak or damaged growth. Cut back any excessively vigorous shoots.

ROUTINE PRUNING
Try to keep the plants balanced by cutting back very vigorous shoots and thinning out any tangled, congested shoots. Remove any broken or damaged shoots when you see them. Thin out congested shoots by removing alternate shoots after flowering. Cut back any strong, vigorous stems by removing the end one-third of each shoot.

REMEDIAL PRUNING
Older plants tend to become bare and leggy at the base, exposing old bark that is marked with deep cracks and fissures. They will usually respond to hard pruning. Cut the plant back to a framework of strong shoots within 1–2ft (30–60cm) above ground level in midspring.

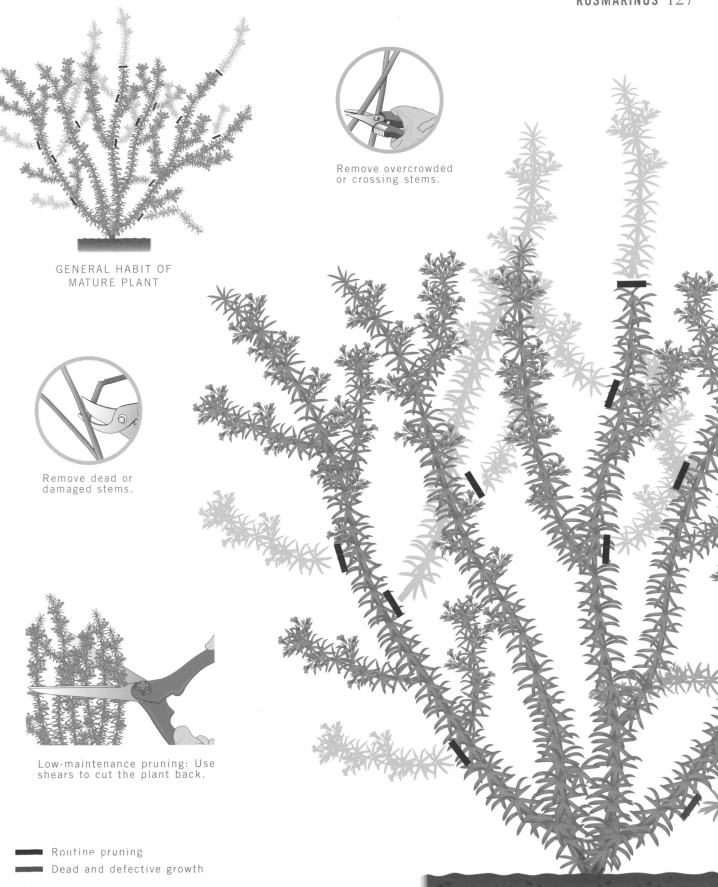

GENERAL HABIT OF
MATURE PLANT

Remove overcrowded
or crossing stems.

Remove dead or
damaged stems.

Low-maintenance pruning: Use
shears to cut the plant back.

▬ Routine pruning
▬ Dead and defective growth

SALIX
Willow

Willows are often grown for their vividly colored stems or for their eye-catching, variegated foliage. Some forms have attractive flowers (catkins), while others are selected for their lax weeping habit or contorted stems and leaves.

WHY PRUNE?
To restrict the plant's height and to promote the production of new, brightly colored shoots.

PRUNING TIPS
- Start pruning just as the buds start to grow.
- Use bypass pruners because anvil-type pruners will easily crush the stems.

WHEN TO PRUNE MOST SPECIES
Early or midspring

PLANTS PRUNED THIS WAY
- *Cornus alba* and cvs.: in midspring
- *Cornus sanguinea* and cvs.: in midspring
- *Cornus stolonifera*: in midspring
- *Salix alba* and cvs.: in early spring; remove deadwood in summer
- *Salix daphnoides*: in early spring; remove deadwood in summer
- *Salix purpurea* and cvs.: in early spring; remove deadwood in summer

WHICH TOOLS
- Hand pruners
- Long-handled pruners (loppers)
- Pruning saw

FORMATIVE PRUNING

Try to encourage the development of a multistemmed plant with strong shoots forming close to ground level. Plants that are to be coppiced (stooled) are cut back hard—to within about 6in (15cm)—after planting in winter or early spring. This will encourage new shoots to develop from the base of the plant as it becomes established. Plants that are to be pollarded are left for the first year to grow a single stem about 3ft (1m) high. Then the growing point is removed in winter or early spring to encourage new shoots to develop from the top of this 3ft (1m) high leg as the plant becomes established.

ROUTINE PRUNING

If they are to produce the most attractive winter colors, these plants need regular annual pruning to remove old wood and encourage new shoots. Pruning should cut out any weak or thin shoots. In spring, cut back the 1-year-old stems as close to the old branch framework as possible. This will leave stubs of growth 1–2in (2.5–5cm) long, from which the new shoots will emerge. If the old stubs of growth have become overcrowded, remove them with a small pruning saw.

REMEDIAL PRUNING

Willows that are left unpruned tend to become a dense mass of thin, weak, straggly stems that produce poor color. The plant will also be more susceptible to pests and diseases. This can be overcome by hard pruning, which can be done in stages over two to three years or by cutting down the plant completely. In winter, cut back all the old stems as close to the old branch framework as possible, using a saw if necessary. Leave stubs 1–2in (2.5–5cm) long, from which the new shoots will emerge. In late spring, completely remove any thin or weak shoots. Cut out any branches that are rubbing or crossing over each other.

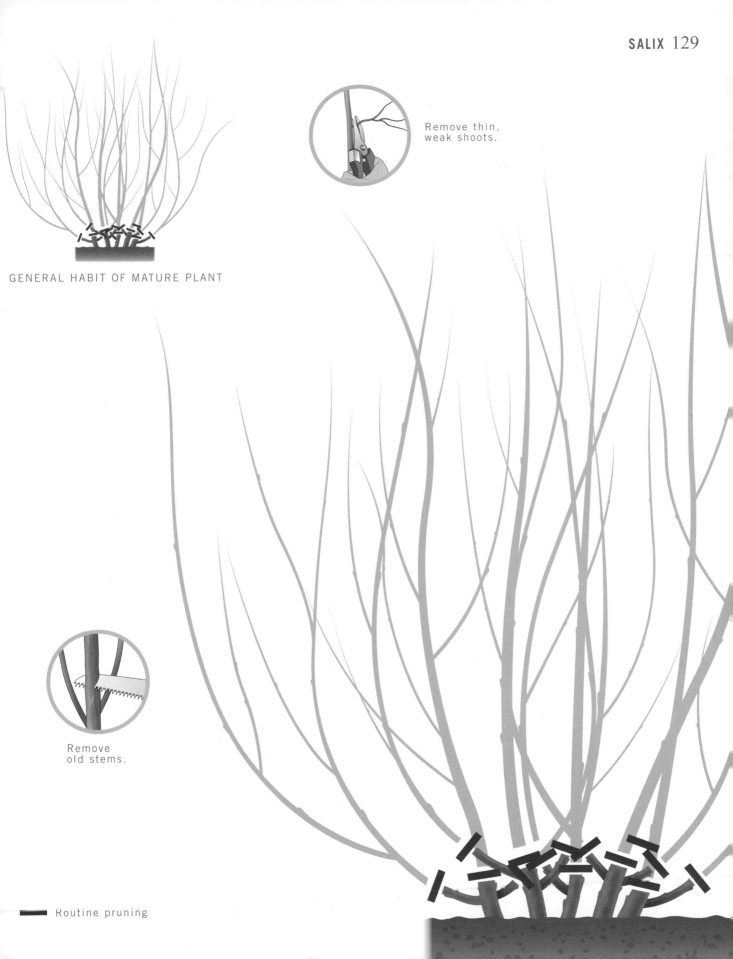

GENERAL HABIT OF MATURE PLANT

Remove thin,
weak shoots.

Remove
old stems.

Routine pruning

SAMBUCUS
Elderberry, elder

Striking foliage, flowers, and berries make elderberries good-value shrubs and trees, especially at home in mixed borders and woodland-style gardens.

WHY PRUNE?

To encourage new, attractive foliage.

PRUNING TIPS

Cut close to the buds to prevent dieback.

WHEN TO PRUNE MOST SPECIES

Winter

PLANTS PRUNED THIS WAY

- *Cornus alba* and cvs.: in midspring
- *Cornus sanguinea* and cvs.: in midspring
- *Salix* spp. and cvs.: in midspring
- *Sambucus nigra* and cvs.: in winter
- *Sambucus racemosa* and cvs.: in winter

WHICH TOOLS

- Hand pruners
- Long-handled pruners (loppers)
- Pruning saw

FORMATIVE PRUNING

Try to develop a multistemmed plant, with strong shoots forming close to ground level. In the winter or early spring after planting, cut plants back hard—to about 6in (15cm). At the same time, remove any thin, weak shoots to encourage new shoots to grow from the base of the plant.

ROUTINE PRUNING

Elders need regular annual pruning if they are to produce the most attractive foliage. Remove the older wood and encourage production of new shoots. Cut out weak, thin shoots. In winter, coppice the plant by cutting back the one-year-old stems as close to the old branch framework as possible, leaving 1–2in (2.5–5cm) stubs of growth from which the new shoots will emerge. Alternatively, remove older growth and cut one-year-old stems by one-third. If the old stubs of growth become overcrowded, remove them with a small pruning saw.

REMEDIAL PRUNING

If they are left unpruned, elderberries become tall and bare at the base with a mass of thin, weak, straggly stems that produce poor foliage size and color. This can be overcome with hard pruning, which involves cutting the plant down completely. In winter, cut back all the old stems as close to the old branch framework as possible, using a saw if necessary and leaving 1–2in (2.5–5cm) stubs of growth from which the new shoots will emerge. In late spring, completely remove any thin or weak new shoots.

GENERAL HABIT OF
MATURE PLANT

Remove thin,
weak growth.

Remove old, congested
stubs of growth.

Remove dead or
damaged stems.

▬ Routine pruning
▬ Dead and defective growth

SPIRAEA 'ARGUTA'

Bridal wreath, foam of May

This hardy shrub often bears so many flowers that they appear to be a layer of foam coating the leaves, giving the plant one of its common names, foam of May.

WHY PRUNE?

To restrict the plant's height and to encourage it to develop a bushy habit.

PRUNING TIPS

- Start pruning before the new shoots form so that you don't lose next year's flowers.
- Use bypass pruners because anvil-type pruners will easily crush the stems.

WHEN TO PRUNE MOST SPECIES

Early summer

PLANTS PRUNED THIS WAY

- *Dipelta* spp. and cvs.: in midsummer, after flowering
- *Forsythia* spp. and cvs.: in mid- to late spring, after flowering
- *Kerria japonica* and cvs.: in late spring, after flowering
- *Spiraea nipponica*: in early summer, after flowering
- *Spiraea japonica*: in very early spring
- *Spiraea ×vanhouttei*: in late spring, after flowering
- *Weigela florida* and cvs.: in midsummer, after flowering

WHICH TOOLS

- Hand pruners

FORMATIVE PRUNING

Young plants should be pruned to encourage a bushy shape with strong shoots emerging from soil level. After planting, remove any old growth. Cut back the remaining shoots to about half their length to encourage the development of new shoots from the base of the plant as it becomes established.

ROUTINE PRUNING

If it is to flower well, this plant needs regular annual pruning to remove the old wood, which would gradually accumulate, and encourage the production of new flower-bearing shoots. Cut back the old flower-bearing stems as close to the ground as possible in early summer to allow the maximum period of growth to produce a good display of flowers the following year. Prune old flower-bearing stems at least halfway along their length, cutting to just above a healthy bud or to a well-placed new sideshoot. Try to remove about one-quarter of the old stems each year to allow in light and make room for new shoots to develop.

REMEDIAL PRUNING

Spiraea 'Arguta' tends to become thick and overcrowded as it ages, especially if the pruning has been neglected, and the resulting thicket of thin, weak, straggly stems will produce few flowers and leave the plant susceptible to pests and diseases. This can be overcome by hard pruning, which must be done in stages rather than by simply cutting the plant down completely. Leaving three or four strong stems, in early summer cut the remaining shoots back to within 2–3in (5–7cm) of ground level to encourage new replacement shoots to develop. The following year, completely remove any thin or weak shoots. Cut out the three or four remaining old stems close to ground level.

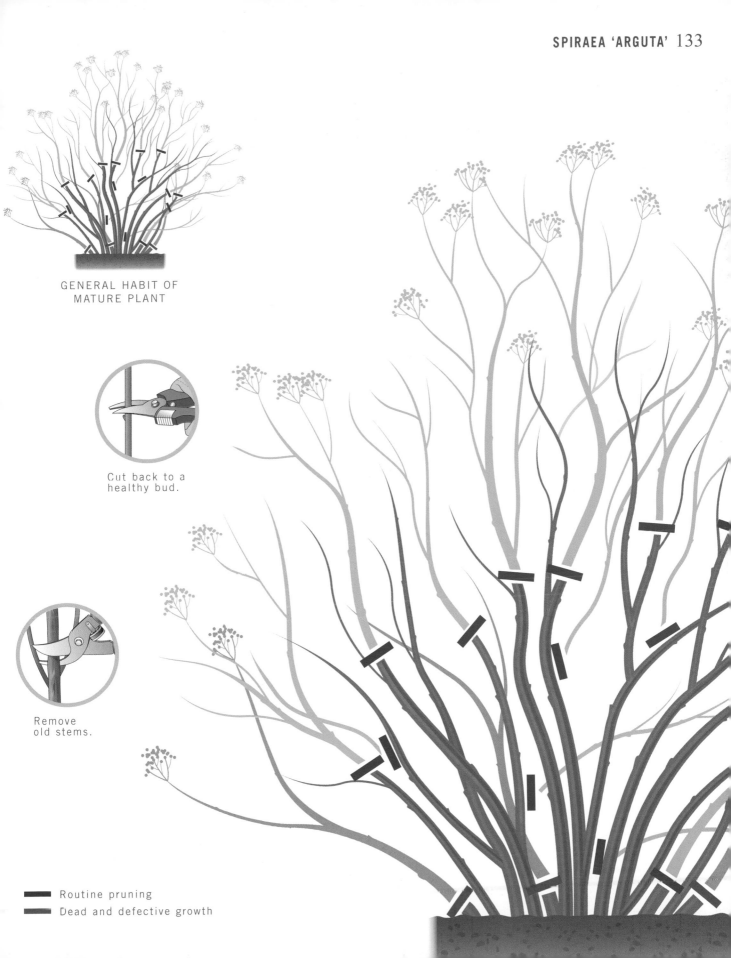

GENERAL HABIT OF
MATURE PLANT

Cut back to a
healthy bud.

Remove
old stems.

Routine pruning
Dead and defective growth

SYRINGA

Lilac

You can rely on lilac to provide a stunning display of late-spring blooms. They are easy-to-grow shrubs that seem to do particularly well in town gardens.

WHY PRUNE?

To promote flowering and to encourage development of new shoots.

PRUNING TIPS

Most lilacs flower on buds formed the previous season. If you choose to remove the fading flowers, take care not to damage the new growth because that produces next year's blooms.

WHEN TO PRUNE MOST SPECIES

Midsummer

PLANTS PRUNED THIS WAY

- *Syringa vulgaris* and cvs.: in midsummer, after flowering
- *Syringa ×josiflexa*: in midsummer, after flowering
- *Syringa ×prestoniae*: in midsummer, after flowering
- *Syringa ×hyacinthiflora*: in midsummer, after flowering

WHICH TOOLS

- Hand pruners
- Long-handled pruners (loppers)

FORMATIVE PRUNING

Prune young plants to encourage them to develop a bushy habit, with strong shoots emerging from just above soil level. These shoots can be trained as a framework onto a supporting structure. In the first spring after planting, cut out any weak or damaged stems. Prune the tips of the main shoots by removing the end one-third of each.

ROUTINE PRUNING

These plants do not need regular annual pruning to flower well, but they should be pruned to avoid long, straggly stems with lots of bare wood and to encourage production of new flower-bearing shoots. Immediately after flowering, cut the old flower-bearing stems back to a strong pair of buds. This will give the maximum period of growth to produce a good display of flowers the following year. Cut back any thin, weak, or overcrowded shoots to a strong pair of buds.

REMEDIAL PRUNING

Left unpruned, lilacs may become overgrown with lots of bare wood. This can be overcome by hard pruning. In winter, cut half of the old stems back to within 18in (45cm) of soil level. Cut out any thin, weak, or unwanted shoots. In the second year, completely cut out any thin or weak shoots and remove any old branches that remain from the previous year. Lilacs are sometimes grafted onto a rootstock. If you know your lilac is grafted, remove any suckers as soon as they are about 12in (30cm) long, or large enough to handle, removing them as close to the main root as possible. Suckers on ungrafted lilacs can be used to rejuvenate the shrub.

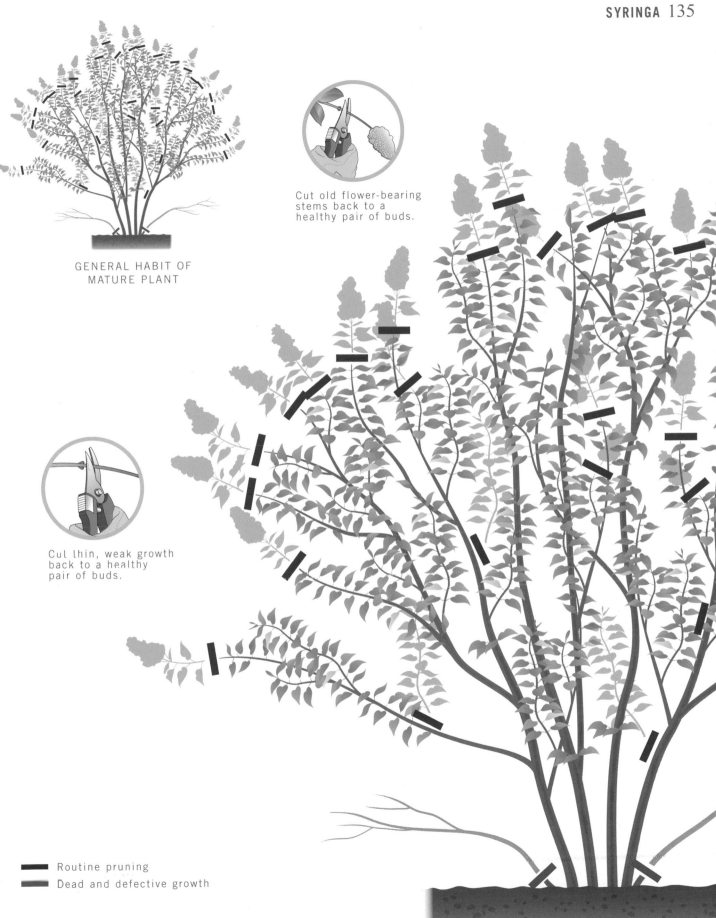

GENERAL HABIT OF
MATURE PLANT

Cut old flower-bearing
stems back to a
healthy pair of buds.

Cut thin, weak growth
back to a healthy
pair of buds.

Routine pruning
Dead and defective growth

TAXUS

English yew, yew

These hardy, long-lived, evergreen plants are especially valued as freestanding specimen trees, but they are also excellent hedging and screening plants.

WHY PRUNE?
To promote even, balanced growth and to remove damaged stems.

PRUNING TIPS
Don't prune in late fall, because young growths will be damaged by frosts.

WHEN TO PRUNE MOST SPECIES
Mid- or late spring

PLANTS PRUNED THIS WAY
- *Taxus* spp. and cvs.: in mid- or late spring
- *Thuja* spp. and cvs.: in mid- or late spring; will not tolerate remedial pruning
- *Tsuga* spp. and cvs.: in mid- or late spring; will not tolerate remedial pruning

WHICH TOOLS
- Hand pruners
- Long-handled pruners (loppers)
- Pruning saw

FORMATIVE PRUNING

Young plants require only light pruning to develop into multistemmed plants (which yews naturally form anyway), with strong shoots forming an evenly balanced framework. In late spring, remove any damaged shoots. Cut back any shoots that are growing across the center of the plants. Prune the remaining shoots lightly by removing the end third of each shoot. Cut back vigorous shoots by about half to keep the growth even and balanced.

ROUTINE PRUNING

Yews tolerate shearing and are therefore thought of primarily as hedge plants. If possible, though, it is better to remove selected shoots with hand pruners than it is to shear the plants; cut back vigorous shoots to balance the growth and shape of the plant. Cut vigorous stems back at least halfway along their length to just above a healthy bud or to a well-placed sideshoot. Remove any thin, weak growth from the center of the plant. Remove any new growth that has been damaged by late frosts.

REMEDIAL PRUNING

As they age, yews produce less extension growth at the tip of each shoot and slowly increase in overall size. At the same time, they may become bare and straggly at the base, or the branches may splay out, leaving an open center. In late spring, cut all the stems back to 18–24in (45–60cm) above soil level. Cut any side branches back to within 1in (2.5cm) of the stems. In summer, remove any thin, overcrowded shoots.

GENERAL HABIT OF
MATURE PLANT

Remove thin,
weak growth.

Remove frost-
damaged stems.

Remove dead or dying stems
to prevent them from rotting
and killing nearby growth.

■ Routine pruning
■ Dead and defective growth

VACCINIUM
Blueberry

These attractive, deciduous shrubs are close relatives of heathers and pieris and complement them very well with their displays of flowers and fruits. Deciduous forms also produce attractive fall leaf color.

WHY PRUNE?
To maintain plant health and vigor and for fruit production.

PRUNING TIPS
For groundcover plants, use shears for light pruning.

WHEN TO PRUNE MOST SPECIES
Late winter

PLANTS PRUNED THIS WAY
- *Ribes* spp and cvs.: in late winter
- *Vaccinium angustifolium*: in late winter
- *Vaccinium corymbosum*: in late winter

WHICH TOOLS
- Hand pruners
- Long-handled pruners (loppers)

FORMATIVE PRUNING

Prune young plants to encourage them to develop a bushy habit, with strong shoots emerging from just above soil level. After planting, remove any weak or damaged growth and cut back the remaining shoots to about half their length to encourage the growth of new shoots at the base of the plant.

ROUTINE PRUNING

Try to produce a compact, bushy framework. Encourage new shoots to prevent the plant from becoming bare at the base. In late winter, trim back any long, vigorous shoots and remove any congested growth.

REMEDIAL PRUNING

These shrubs become overcrowded as they age, with a lot of thin, weak, straggly stems producing fewer, smaller flowers. This can be overcome by hard pruning, but the following season's flowers and fruit will be lost. In late winter or early spring, cut the old, strong shoots back to within 4–6in (10–15cm) of ground level, and cut out any thin, weak growth to encourage the growth of new shoots.

GENERAL HABIT OF
MATURE PLANT

Cut back
overvigorous
stems.

Remove overcrowded
or crossing stems.

▬ Routine pruning
▬ Dead and defective growth

VIBURNUM
(deciduous species)
Viburnum

Viburnums are ideal for small gardens, offering year-round interest from the foliage, flowers, and fruit. They are also easy to grow.

WHY PRUNE?

To promote a well-balanced, open shape and the production of new stems.

PRUNING TIPS

Don't deadhead if you want a display of fruits.

WHEN TO PRUNE MOST SPECIES

Late winter

PLANTS PRUNED THIS WAY

- *Viburnum carlesii*: in late winter
- *Viburnum dentatum*: in late winter
- *Viburnum dilatatum*: in late winter
- *Viburnum farreri*: in late winter
- *Viburnum ×juddii*: in late winter
- *Viburnum opulus*: in late winter
- *Viburnum trilobum*: in late winter

WHICH TOOLS

- Hand pruners
- Long-handled pruners (loppers)
- Pruning saw

FORMATIVE PRUNING

Plants should be allowed to develop naturally. Pruning may be necessary to prevent them from becoming unbalanced. After planting, cut out any weak or damaged growth. Cut back any excessively vigorous shoots.

ROUTINE PRUNING

Many viburnums are grown for their berries; it is important to note that if they are deadheaded, the plants will not produce berries. Prune viburnums to control size, or to remove the old wood that would gradually accumulate, and to encourage new flower-bearing shoots. Viburnums require only light pruning, so remove about one-fifth of the old stems each year to allow light in and to make room for new shoots. Cut out any thin, weak shoots and any congested, crossing branches to reduce rubbing.

REMEDIAL PRUNING

If they are left unpruned, viburnums can become overcrowded, with a mass of thin, weak, straggly stems that produce poor stem color and make them susceptible to pests and diseases. This can be overcome by cutting the plant down completely. In late spring, cut back all old stems close to ground level, using a saw if necessary and leaving 1–2in (2.5–5cm) stubs of woody stem from which the new shoots will emerge. In summer, completely remove any thin or weak shoots.

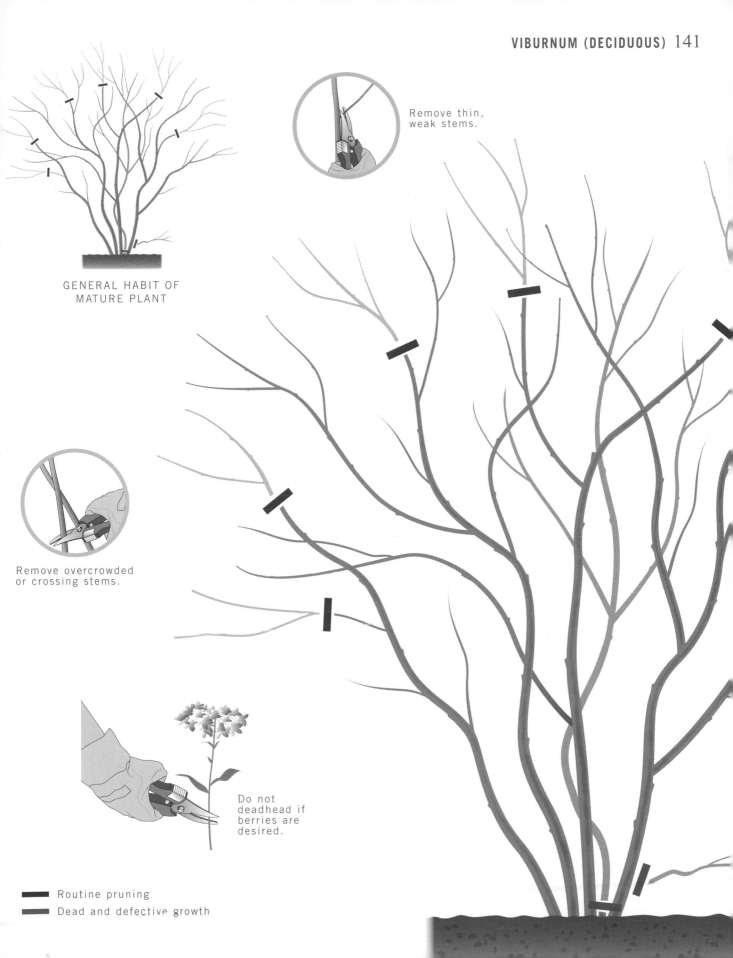

GENERAL HABIT OF
MATURE PLANT

Remove thin,
weak stems.

Remove overcrowded
or crossing stems.

Do not
deadhead if
berries are
desired.

Routine pruning

Dead and defective growth

VIBURNUM
(evergreen and semi-evergreen species)
Viburnum

Evergreen and semi-evergreen viburnums have glossy green leaves, which provide a handsome background for the fragrant flowers.

WHY PRUNE?
To maintain a well-balanced, open shape and to encourage the production of new stems.

PRUNING TIPS
Keep a watch for sucker growth and remove it as soon as possible.

WHEN TO PRUNE MOST SPECIES
Early or midsummer

PLANTS PRUNED THIS WAY
- *Viburnum betulifolium*: in spring, after flowering
- *Viburnum ×burkwoodii*: in summer, after flowering
- *Viburnum davidii*: in summer, after flowering
- *Viburnum rhytidophyllum*: in summer, after flowering
- *Viburnum tinus*: in summer, after flowering

WHICH TOOLS
- Hand pruners
- Long-handled pruners (loppers)
- Pruning saw

FORMATIVE PRUNING

Try to develop a multistemmed plant, with strong shoots forming close to ground level. In the spring after planting, lightly prune the shoots by removing about one-third of each shoot. This will encourage stocky, bushy plants. Cut back vigorous shoots by about half their length to keep the plant's growth even and balanced.

ROUTINE PRUNING

These plants do not require regular pruning to keep growing well, but they will do better if any vigorous shoots are pruned back to balance the growth and shape. After flowering, the plant can be deadheaded by cutting the old flower-bearing clusters back to a strong bud or down to lower, stronger shoots. Many viburnums are grown for their berries; it is important to note that if they are deadheaded, the plants will not produce berries. Prune vigorous stems to at least half their length, cutting back to just above a healthy bud or to a well-placed sideshoot. Remove any thin, weak growth emerging from the center of the plant.

REMEDIAL PRUNING

As they age, these plants become congested and produce fewer flowers. They often become bare and straggly at the base. In late spring, cut all the main stems back to 1–2ft (30–60cm) above ground level. Remove any thin, overcrowded, or crossing shoots.

GENERAL HABIT OF
MATURE PLANT

Remove
overvigorous
stems.

Remove dead
flowers.

Remove thin,
weak growth.

Routine pruning
Dead and defective growth

VITIS
Grape vine, vine

This is one of the most rewarding climbers to grow if you want a display of fiery fall colors. Before they drop, the leaves of these vigorous plants turn to brilliant shades of red, crimson, or bright purple.

WHY PRUNE?
To produce balanced growth, to control vigor, and for fruit production.

PRUNING TIPS
Prune in winter or when the plant is in full leaf to minimize the likelihood of excessive bleeding.

WHEN TO PRUNE MOST SPECIES
Late winter

PLANTS PRUNED THIS WAY
- *Vitis amurensis* and cvs.: in late winter, before sap begins to rise
- *Vitis coignetiae* and cvs.: in late winter, before sap begins to rise
- *Vitis vinifera* and cvs.: in late winter, before sap begins to rise

WHICH TOOLS
- Hand pruners
- Long-handled pruners (loppers)

FORMATIVE PRUNING

Prune young plants to encourage them to develop a framework of strong shoots emerging from just above soil level. In the first winter after planting, remove any weak or damaged growth, cutting back to a strong, healthy bud 18in (45cm) above ground level. As new shoots develop, select three or four of the strongest ones for training into the supporting structure. In the second winter, cut the tips of these shoots back by about one-quarter and train them into the support structure. Cut any thin shoots back to one or two buds and remove the weakest shoots altogether.

ROUTINE PRUNING

Try to maintain a framework of strong, healthy shoots and encourage formation of more healthy shoots. Mature plants are also pruned to keep them within their allotted space. In late winter, shorten the main stems by cutting them back as needed. Tie them into place on the support structure. Cut the sideshoots back to within two or three buds of their point of origin. Remove any shoots that are not needed to prevent overcrowding. In summer, remove any overcrowded shoots. Cut out any old, bare stems close to ground level to make room for new growth.

REMEDIAL PRUNING

As vines age, they often become a tangled mass of old and new growth; this overcrowding often causes poor, weak stems. They will respond to hard pruning, however. In winter, cut the plant back to a framework of three or four main stems about 3ft (1m) long. After the plant rejuvenates, remove all the weak, thin shoots, leaving up to four of the strongest, healthiest shoots to form a new framework. Train these into position.

GENERAL HABIT OF
MATURE PLANT

Tie in main
growth.

FORMATIVE PRUNING

Second winter

Remove overcrowded
or crossing stems.

▬ Routine pruning
▬ Dead and defective growth

WEIGELA

Weigela

Weigelas are among the most popular shrubs in the modern garden. They are easy to grow and will perform well over many years with little or no attention. They are often planted close to forsythia, as they flower soon afterward.

WHY PRUNE?
To keep a well-balanced shape and to encourage the plant to develop a bushy habit.

PRUNING TIPS
Use bypass hand pruners because the stems will be easily crushed by anvil-type hand pruners.

WHEN TO PRUNE MOST SPECIES
Midsummer

PLANTS PRUNED THIS WAY
- *Dipelta* spp. and cvs.: in midsummer, after flowering
- *Forsythia* spp. and cvs.: in mid- to late spring, after flowering
- *Kerria japonica* and cvs.: in late spring, after flowering
- *Weigela* spp. and cvs.: in midsummer, after flowering

WHICH TOOLS
- Hand pruners
- Long-handled pruners (loppers)

FORMATIVE PRUNING
Prune young plants to encourage them to grow bushy, with strong shoots emerging from ground level. After planting, remove any damaged growth. Cut the remaining shoots back to about half of their length to encourage development of new shoots from the base of the plant as it becomes established.

ROUTINE PRUNING
If it is to flower well, this plant needs regular annual pruning to remove the old wood that would gradually accumulate, and to encourage production of new flower-bearing shoots. Cut back old flower-bearing stems at least halfway along their length to just above a healthy bud or to a well-placed new sideshoot. Remove or shorten overvigorous new growth that ruins the shape of the plant. Aim to remove about one-quarter of the old stems each year to allow in light and make room for new shoots.

REMEDIAL PRUNING
Weigelas often become thick and congested as they age, with a thicket of thin, weak, straggly stems producing few flowers, especially if the pruning has been neglected. This can be overcome by cutting the plant down completely. In early spring, cut the old growth back to within 2–3in (5–7cm) of ground level to encourage new shoots to replace the old ones. In midsummer, completely remove any thin or weak shoots. Prune back the three or four remaining old stems, cutting close to ground level.

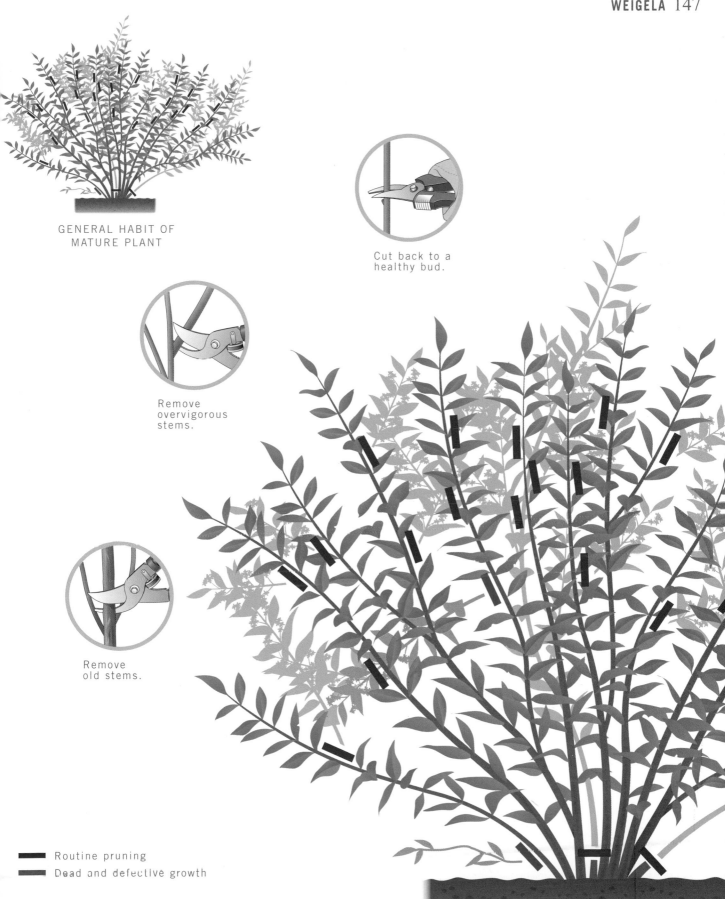

GENERAL HABIT OF
MATURE PLANT

Cut back to a
healthy bud.

Remove
overvigorous
stems.

Remove
old stems.

▬ Routine pruning
═ Dead and defective growth

WISTERIA

Wisteria

Few sights are more impressive than that of a mature wisteria in full flower. The trailing clusters of pealike blooms are one of the highlights of the late spring or summer garden.

WHY PRUNE?

To create a strong framework for the large, pendulous flowers.

PRUNING TIPS

- Look at the plant carefully before pruning and decide exactly what it is you want to achieve.
- Be brave and decisive. Wisteria is rarely harmed.

WHEN TO PRUNE MOST SPECIES

Late winter and midsummer

PLANTS PRUNED THIS WAY

- *Wisteria brachybotrys* and cvs.: in late winter and midsummer, after flowering
- *Wisteria floribunda* and cvs.: in late winter and midsummer, after flowering
- *Wisteria* ×*formosa* and cvs.: in late winter and midsummer, after flowering
- *Wisteria sinensis* and cvs.: in late winter and midsummer, after flowering

WHICH TOOLS

- Hand pruners
- Pruning knife

FORMATIVE PRUNING

After planting, stake and cut back the leader to a healthy bud 3ft (1m) above ground level. Remove all laterals and sideshoots. In the first summer, tie in the vertical leader, then select two strong laterals and tie in at 45 degrees. Prune sideshoots to about 6in (15cm) or three or four buds to begin formation of flowering spurs. Remove any shoots emanating from the base of the plant. In the first summer, cut back the leader to about 3ft (1m) above laterals. Pull down laterals previously trained at 45 degrees and tie in horizontally. Cut back by a third of their length. In the second summer, tie in the leader and horizontal laterals as they grow. Prune sideshoots to three or four buds. Select the next pair of laterals and tie in at a 45-degree angle. Again remove any basal growth. In the second winter, cut back the leader and tie in laterals as in previous winter pruning. Prune back laterals by about one-third of their length to ripe wood. Continue this sequence until the available space is covered.

PRUNING THE MATURE PLANT

Once the desired space has been filled, the established plant is pruned solely to restrain spread and create further flowering spurs. Rapid extension growths will soon make a tangled mass of whip-like shoots if left uncurtailed, and these must be cut back each summer to form the spurs on which the following year's flowers will appear. The more frequently these growths are cut back, the more congested the flowering spurs become, and dedicated growers will prune them back to 6in (15cm) every two weeks during the summer once flowering has finished. The spurs are shortened to two or three buds on each shoot in the winter prune, at which time the plump flower buds are easily distinguished from the flattened growth buds. This gives the gardener a good advance indication of the following season's flowering potential.

FORMATIVE PRUNING

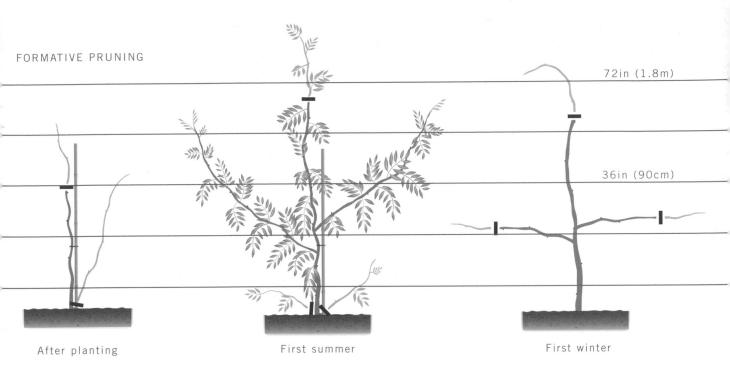

72in (1.8m)

36in (90cm)

After planting

First summer

First winter

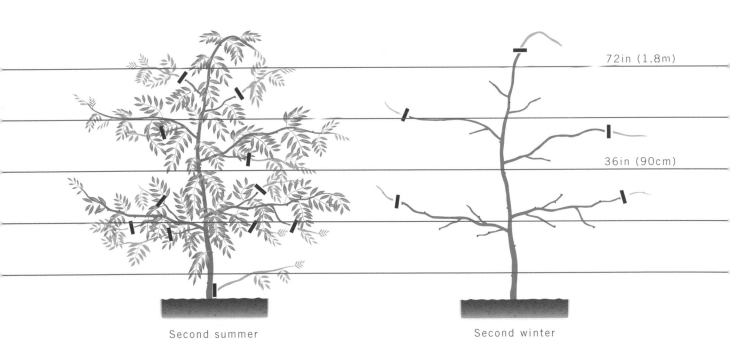

72in (1.8m)

36in (90cm)

Second summer

Second winter

▬ Routine pruning

SUMMER PRUNING
After all flowering has finished,
prune all new shoots back to
6in (15cm), or four to six leaves,
from the main branch. Repeated
cutting back of these shoots
will result over time in thickly
congested spurs producing a
profusion of flowers in spring
and early summer.

Routine pruning

Tie in new growth.

WINTER PRUNING
When the plant is dormant in winter, further shorten the spurs to within 3–4in (7–10cm) of their parent branch, leaving two to three buds on each spur shoot. Flower buds are plump, dark, and slightly hairy, and are easily distinguished at this stage from the flatter growth buds.

SPECIAL FEATURES

This section includes features on hedging, renovation pruning, and low-maintenance pruning. More specialized pruning techniques such as pollarding, pleaching, and topiary are also discussed. Quick-reference tables at the end show when to prune your plants and provide a list of plants requiring little or no pruning.

TREES

We plant trees in our gardens to provide the illusion of permanence and the reality of structure. Trees will probably be the longest-lived plants we ever select and grow, and because of this, we tend to assume they can take care of themselves with little or no help or guidance.

In a garden, a tree can serve several purposes, including providing shade and shelter or attractive foliage or flowers and fruits; we may need to manage it to suit these requirements. Trees that produce attractive juvenile foliage or brightly colored young stems in winter need regular pruning so that their most attractive feature is prominent. Even routine pruning to remove diseased or damaged limbs or branches will help to extend the life of a tree by many years. Selecting the correct time of year to prune certain trees can also help keep them strong and healthy.

Most deciduous trees are pruned in winter during their dormancy, but for some, pruning at this time can be a messy proposition: *Acer* spp. (maple), *Betula* spp. (birch), and *Juglans* spp. (walnut) bleed copious quantities of sap if they are pruned in late winter or early spring. Types of *Prunus* (cherries and their relatives) are also often pruned in summer to avoid the incidence of fungal diseases, especially silver leaf, which are less prevalent in the growing season.

FORMATIVE PRUNING

Formative pruning of ornamental trees often occurs in the nursery before the plants are offered for sale. The young trees you buy have usually been trained to develop a straight stem and well-spaced branches for a structural framework that should last throughout the tree's lifetime.

Some plants are more difficult to train than others, particularly plants with leaves and buds arranged

PRODUCING A SINGLE-STEMMED TREE
After planting, remove the lowest branches. Cut out any top shoots that are competing with the main stem.

As the tree develops, remove lower branches flush with the main stem and cut the branches immediately above back to about 4in (10cm).

Repeat the process in subsequent years, removing the lowest branches and reducing the ones immediately above in length, before removing them completely the following year.

As the top or head of the tree develops, trim the branches back to form a balanced structure.

Choose a multistemmed shape for variety in your garden. Many trees and large shrubs look more attractive if grown as a multistemmed plant.

along the stems in opposite pairs—such as *Acer* (maple), *Aesculus* (horse chestnut), and *Fraxinus* (ash)—because they often fork and develop two main stems. The problem will arise in later years when the stems split, causing huge wounds and severe structural damage to the trees, as well as a strong potential for fungal rots.

Prune deciduous shade-producing and flowering trees in the first three years to produce a clear stem for the tree and to create an open, well-balanced framework of branches—the crown or the head. It is important to produce a structure that gives each branch plenty of space and light. Also remove competing or rubbing branches.

In late spring or early summer, remove any shoots emerging from the trunk below the branches in the head of the tree because these will compete with the main stem. Cut back by two-thirds

or remove altogether any overcrowded or competing shoots in the head of the tree to prevent branches from crossing and rubbing.

Always cut back to an outward-facing bud or shoot so that new shoots do not grow back into the center of the branch network.

PRODUCING A MULTISTEMMED TREE Allow the tree to grow for one year before cutting the main stem down to about 6in (15cm) above soil level.

Allow three or four strong shoots to grow.

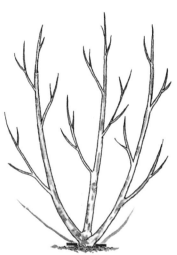

As the new shoots develop and form strong stems, remove any thin, weak shoots that emerge at the base of the plant.

ROUTINE PRUNING

Many established ornamental and shade-producing trees require little routine pruning beyond removing shoots to keep the crown open and tidy and to keep the lower sections of the trunk clear. Severe pruning may, in fact, provoke the tree to produce excessive growth in the form of sappy water (epicormic) shoots. If these are not cut off before they become too large, they will scar the tree trunk when they are eventually removed.

As a tree matures, it may develop an overcrowded head or crown congested with thin, whippy branches in the center. Some branch thinning may be necessary to allow light and air into the center of the tree. Also, as the branches age, some species may tend to droop toward the ground, and some of the lower branches may need to be shortened or removed altogether. Occasionally, a large branch that spoils the balance and shape of the tree may need to be shortened or removed.

In late spring or early summer, cut out any dead, dying, diseased, and damaged wood. This type of growth is much easier to see while the tree is growing rather than in winter when the plant is dormant. Remove any stem and root suckers. Cut any water shoots off flush with the stem. Prune out or cut back any crossing or overcrowded branches to an outward-facing bud. Reduce in length any large branches that spoil the balance of the tree's head (crown).

REMOVING BRANCHES

There may be times when larger branches must be removed from a mature tree. These branches are likely to be heavy, and for safety you should remove them in several sections. Before you begin, make sure that removing one or more branches will not damage the remainder of the tree, which you want to continue to grow after pruning.

There is a procedure that ensures safe removal of large branches by reducing the weight of the branch before you make the final cut. Although it involves extra cutting, the saw will not usually get caught in the pruning cut and the branch will not tear away when partly cut, injuring the trunk as it falls to the ground.

Rather than immediately cutting the branch off close to the trunk, make an undercut on the underside of the branch at a convenient distance along the branch away from the

ROUTINE PRUNING
For most single-stemmed trees, remove any shoots emerging on the main stem and cut out any shoots growing across the head of the tree.

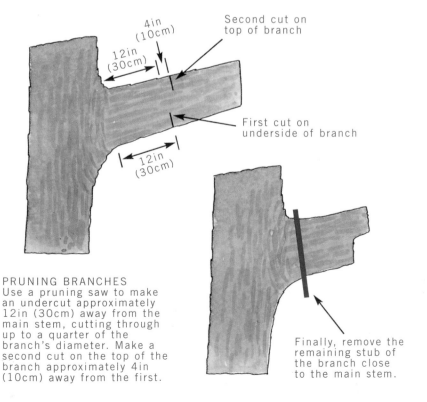

PRUNING BRANCHES
Use a pruning saw to make an undercut approximately 12in (30cm) away from the main stem, cutting through up to a quarter of the branch's diameter. Make a second cut on the top of the branch approximately 4in (10cm) away from the first.

4in (10cm)

12in (30cm)

12in (30cm)

Second cut on top of branch

First cut on underside of branch

Finally, remove the remaining stub of the branch close to the main stem.

Most mature trees require little pruning. Simply remove any untidy shoots and keep the base of the trunk clear.

POST-PRUNING
Remove any strong, new shoots that emerge close to the old pruning point.

trunk. Make a second cut on the top of the branch and farther out along the branch from the first cut but parallel to it. As this second cut reaches the point where it overlaps the first cut, the branch will snap along the grain and should fall clear. This technique is called a "jump cut." Finally, remove the remaining stump of the branch close to the branch's shoulder—the swollen area at the base of the branch where it joins the trunk. Cutting at this point allows the most rapid healing of the wound caused by branch removal.

Use a suitable saw and start by making an undercut about 12in (30cm) away from the trunk. Cut up to a quarter of the way through the branch. Make the second cut on the top of the branch and 4in (10cm) farther along the branch (away from the trunk). Remove the remaining stub close to the trunk.

REMEDIAL PRUNING

Trees may outgrow their allotted space, be damaged by weather, or become unsafe with age, and it is sometimes necessary to remove a tree altogether and plant a new one. Replacement may be the only option, especially if safety is a concern. Contact a qualified arborist (tree surgeon) for advice and guidance.

Remedial pruning is worth doing on trees that are not too old or unsafe. On mature trees extensive remedial pruning is best carried out over several years; remember that in the year following severe pruning, healthy trees may produce large amounts of sappy new growth that will need to be thinned out to prevent congestion. This type of pruning may also provoke production of sucker growths and water shoots. These will also have to be removed to direct the vigor of the tree into areas that need to be developed, such as the branch framework.

In winter, start by cutting out or reducing the length of any branches that are crossing or rubbing. Thin out any congested growths to balance the tree's branch framework. In the second year after starting the remedial pruning, thin out any excessive new growth to prevent congestion. Identify the branches needed to form the framework for the head of the tree. Remove any suckers and water shoots as they emerge.

STANDARD TREES

Despite the many types of trees available from plant nurseries, the most popular form for many gardens is still a standard tree, which has a clear, bare stem with no branches up to a height of about 6ft (2m) above soil level.

A tree of this type can, of course, be readily bought from a nursery or garden center. But some gardeners relish the challenge and sense of achievement that comes from buying a young plant about 5ft (1.5m) high and creating their own standard. This requires a different type of pruning, which must take place in stages over several years to build the stem of the tree and the framework of branches that forms the crown or head. The branches that develop on the trunk of the young tree must be reduced and then removed in stages to allow the trunk to thicken naturally so that it can support the crown. They should not be allowed to become so large that they leave open wounds when removed.

FORMATIVE PRUNING

In the winter or early spring after planting, remove any shoots that are competing with the main stem. This will allow a strong, upright leading shoot to form. In late spring, remove all the sideshoots from the bottom third of the stem. Cut these off as close to the stem (trunk) as possible. At the same time, cut back by half all the sideshoots on the central third of the tree, leaving the top third to develop naturally.

In the second winter after planting, remove completely all the sideshoots from the central third of the tree—these are the shoots that were shortened by half during the previous spring. In spring, cut back by half all the sideshoots on the upper third of the tree. Cut back by half any new branches that have developed in the upper section of the tree. Leave the top section to develop naturally. This process of removing the lower branches can be repeated each year until a clear stem of 6ft (2m) has formed.

FORMATIVE PRUNING
OF STANDARD TREES
After planting a young tree, remove the lowest branches and cut out damaged shoots from the crown.

As the tree develops, remove the lower branches and cut back the branches immediately above this area to about 4in (10cm) in length.

In the following years, systematically remove the lowest branches and reduce the branches immediately above in stages to strengthen the trunk of the tree.

Half and quarter standards may be produced in contrast to the true 6ft (2m) standard stem.

Standard stems are not naturally produced and must be created by careful pruning while the tree is quite young.

CONIFERS

Conifers of all types are among the mainstays of gardens because they provide color and shape throughout the year and, most importantly, require little specialist care. However, as with all plants, they will repay careful pruning, especially in the early years.

We tend to think of conifers as evergreen plants with narrow or needlelike leaves. There are, however, exceptions, and several conifers actually shed their leaves in fall. *Ginkgo biloba* (maidenhair tree), *Larix* spp. (larch), *Metasequoia glyptostroboides* (dawn redwood), and *Taxodium* spp. (swamp cypress) are sometimes referred to as deciduous conifers because they shed their leaves or needles in fall and produce new foliage the following spring.

Most true conifers go through two surges of growth each year: one in spring (the main growth period) and a second (lesser) one in late summer. Pruning just before these growth periods allows the plant to respond quickly to any training and shaping. If they are pruned while they are actively growing, many conifers bleed for long periods, producing large quantities of resin from the open pruning wounds.

Some erect and fastigiate conifers naturally develop a multistemmed habit yet maintain their shape. However, as they age, these plants may spread or splay, getting an open center and losing their attractive profile. Such plants will need remedial pruning.

FORMATIVE PRUNING

The basic growth pattern of conifers such as *Abies* spp. (fir), *Picea* spp. (spruce), and *Pinus* spp. (pine) is a single, central shoot with intermittent clusters of leafy shoots along its length. The central shoot usually becomes the main stem, and the leafy shoots become branches. Some conifers develop a stiff and erect central shoot at an early age, but on others the shoot tip is curved and drooping, becoming erect lower down the stem only as the woody tissue develops. Such plants should be left to grow naturally. Pruning or training is necessary only if the shoots are damaged.

Some conifers develop a second strong shoot close to the top of the plant, and this may compete with the main stem. It is important to remove the growing tip of a competing leader to prevent it from forming a forked stem, which may split and damage the structure of the tree.

In late spring, remove any strong shoots competing with the growing point. If necessary, train a strong vertical shoot against a cane to establish a definite main stem. Remove or cut back by two-thirds any shoots that are capable of competing with the main stem.

Shape conifers by trimming new growth back lightly and cutting back any shoots that compete with the main stem.

Minimal pruning is required for those
conifers that naturally form a conical
or pyramidal habit. Often the only work
required is to trim back any shoots that
splay out from the main branches.

A wide range of shapes
and a huge variety
of foliage colors are
available. Pruning of
most mature conifers
can be restricted to
removing dead, dying,
or damaged growth.

Slow-growing conifers
with a spreading,
prostrate pattern
of growth require
little pruning.

ROUTINE PRUNING

Conifers grow best with minimal pruning. All shapes and sizes are available, so if the plant selected has an appropriate growth habit, there is little need for much routine pruning as the plant matures. Certainly, most pruning on mature conifers is to repair damage or irregular growth that could affect the plant's shape, balance, or stability. However, there are times when the leading shoot, which eventually forms the main stem or even just the growing point, is damaged or dies, and one or more shoots from the top cluster of branches will naturally begin to replace it. A problem arises if two or more branches compete to become the main shoot. When this happens, a forked head may develop. The fork is a weak point, and the tree may split when it is older.

As soon as you see the need for a replacement main stem, select the best-placed strong shoot from the upper cluster of branches and start training it to grow vertically to replace the damaged one. Any competing shoots should be reduced by a third of their length or cut out altogether to establish natural dominance in the replacement main stem.

Pruning of mature conifers should be restricted to removing badly damaged, dying, or dead branches or lower branches that trail on the floor or spoil the plant's natural shape. Attempts to reduce or restrict the height of a mature conifer with an upright habit are usually unsatisfactory and often result in an ugly, mutilated plant—several of the upper branches may grow out at odd angles from the main stem. When this happens, it is better to remove the plant and replace it with a new specimen.

In early spring, remove any dead, dying, diseased, or damaged branches. Lightly trim the tips of vigorous shoots to encourage branching and keep the growth balanced. On *Pinus* spp. (pine) pruning is seldom necessary, but by snapping up to two-thirds of the length of the soft new extension growths—candles—by hand, you will promote denser growth.

REMEDIAL PRUNING

Few conifers can produce new growth from old, bare wood, and they will not respond to remedial pruning. You should dig out any old, damaged, or neglected conifers and replace them. However, *Taxus* spp. (yew) responds positively to severe pruning and can be successfully renovated. *Thuja* spp. (arborvitae) can also be severely pruned, but it will not resprout from bare wood.

Conifers are available in a wide range of shapes and habit and can be slow growing or quite vigorous. Some popular types are shrubby with a spreading or prostrate pattern of growth. Many slow-growing conifers need little pruning unless the plant has been damaged and foliage or branches have to be removed. However, these plants, as with all evergreens, shed some of their old leaves in summer, and the dead leaves often accumulate within the existing foliage and branches. As this dead foliage builds up, it can start to ferment and rot, killing nearby younger leaves and branches and causing sections of the plant to turn brown and die. At least once each summer, inspect the plants and remove the discarded foliage to prevent this type of damage and reduce the need for remedial pruning. Always prune dead branches when the foliage is dry to avoid spreading fungal diseases.

Sometimes a dwarf conifer attempts to revert to a standard-size plant by sending out a fast-growing or larger limb. These rogue shoots must be removed or the dwarf cultivar will quickly be overwhelmed by the faster-growing reversion.

Routine pruning of conifers generally consists of cutting the growing point of each side shoot back to encourage branching.

HEDGES

Hedges play a vital role in our gardens. In addition to marking boundaries and keeping out intruders, they form a backdrop for other plants and features, help to frame a view, and even create screens to hide or divide different parts of the garden.

In many respects, a hedge is a natural-looking barrier created artificially. The individual plants are not allowed to develop their characteristic forms and habits of growth, but instead are treated collectively to fulfill a specific purpose. Trimming and clipping make what may be a disparate selection of plants work together as a unit; frequently cutting back soft, young growths instead of regularly pruning woody stems—as is done with most specimen plants—forces the plants to grow in a particular way. Fortunately for the gardener, many deciduous and evergreen trees and shrubs respond to this frequent cutting by producing an even covering of dense, compact growth.

Hedge clipping is simply a different type of pruning, done in a certain way to achieve a particular purpose. The same general principles that apply to pruning individual plants also govern hedge maintenance. Hedges can be divided into two main groups: formal and informal. There is a third type—the tapestry or mixed hedge—that needs special attention.

Low, formal hedges have traditionally been used to form divisions within a garden. They require regular maintenance, but the ornamental effect is well worth the effort.

Create a stepped effect with closely clipped hedges of varying heights to provide interest in a formal garden.

FORMAL HEDGES

Hedges that require regular clipping or trimming for growth restriction and shape maintenance are known as formal hedges. They are often created from a single species—*Taxus* (yew) or *Fagus* (beech), for example—and they provide the perfect backdrop for ornamental plants and features in a formal setting or in a garden with symmetrical or geometrically shaped beds and borders. In many respects, these hedges are but one step removed from topiary—in fact, topiary shapes are often combined into them as points of interest.

INFORMAL HEDGES

An informal hedge may consist of a single species, and it is likely to be found in a country garden or in one with a relaxed planting style and irregularly shaped and sited beds and borders. How and when informal hedges are pruned depends on the species that make up the hedge and when they flower. In general, informal hedges need less intensive management than formal ones because their pruning is limited to what will encourage flowering. They are usually pruned soon after flowering—removing the old, flower-bearing branches encourages the development of new shoots. Limited pruning means that there are times of the year when this type of hedge may look rather untidy. But this disadvantage is, for many gardeners, outweighed by the reduced amount of work it takes to achieve and maintain an attractive hedge.

Some of the plants in both formal and informal hedges may produce fruits such as hips or berries; the timing of pruning may need slight adjustment so that colorful fruits are not cut off before their display has ended.

TAPESTRY HEDGES

Pruning the third type of hedge, the tapestry or mixed hedge, can be complicated. These hedges consist of more than one species of plant, selected to provide a range of visual interest as the plants change with the seasons. There may be a mixture of plants with different flowering times, leaf colors, and textures, or a combination of evergreen and deciduous species. Wherever it is grown, this type of hedge becomes a feature in its own right as well as providing a colorful background.

Complications arise when it comes to pruning, because no two plants have exactly the same habit and rate of growth. You therefore have to adopt pruning techniques, methods, and timings that are slightly different from those used for single-species hedges.

To make life easier, if you are planting a new tapestry hedge, choose plants with similar growth rates. If you do not, the more vigorous plants will outgrow their weaker neighbors and eventually take over the hedge, spoiling the effect you want to achieve. Careful plant selection makes it possible to have both formal and informal tapestry hedges.

FORMATIVE PRUNING AND TRAINING

The success of a hedge often depends on how it is treated in the first two or three years after planting. Early-stage pruning is critical for any hedge or windbreak so that growth is distributed evenly at the base and at the top. Plants that grow close together in such an unnatural way tend to grow upright fairly rapidly because they are competing with their immediate neighbors. Lack of early-stage formative pruning can lead to unattractive gaps at the base of the hedge that may prevent it from becoming an effective screen or barrier.

Most hedging plants benefit greatly from being cut back immediately after planting. This not only stimulates a dense, bushy habit but also encourages individual plants to grow into one another to form a single unit—the hedge.

Depending on the species used and its habit of growth, after planting it is usual to cut the plants down to about two-thirds of their original height. At the same time, cut back by about half any strong lateral branches that are growing out at right angles to the hedge. This process may be repeated annually for several years to check the amount of growth on the top and sides of the hedge. Most of the new growth will then form between the individual plants, forcing them to grow into one another.

Formative pruning

Year 1 Immediately after planting, cut deciduous plants back to between half and two-thirds of their original height. Remove at least 6in (15cm) of the growing tip of evergreens and conifers. In mid- to late summer, cut out the growing point of any overly vigorous plants as the new shoots develop. Trim back any shoots growing out at right angles to the hedge to create a thick, bushy habit and to keep the plants growing vertically.

Year 2 In the second winter, cut all new growth back by about a third and shorten any laterals growing out at right angles to the hedge. As new shoots develop, lightly trim them back in late spring and early summer to keep the plants bushy and growing upright. Cut back the growing points of any vigorous plants to prevent them from dominating neighboring plants.

ROUTINE PRUNING

Frequently pruning young shoots creates a hedge that is covered with growth over its entire surface. If a hedge is well clipped—especially in the early stages—most species will stay no more than 3ft (1m) wide at the base. The width of the hedge, particularly at the top, is important when it comes to clipping, simply because the wider the hedge the more difficult it is to cut neatly. Hedges that become too wide can also take up garden space valuable for other, more interesting species.

FORMATIVE PRUNING
Year 1: Immediately after planting, cut the plants back hard.

Year 1 (mid- to late summer): As new shoots develop, trim those growing at right angles to the hedge.

Year 2 (winter): Cut new shoots back by about a third.

Year 2 (spring and summer): Trim new shoots and cut out the growing point of any overvigorous shoots.

If you have a formal hedge, aim for one of two shapes. It should be either the same width from bottom to top, or, preferably, narrower at the top than at the base. This sloping angle is known as the batter, and the slope has some practical applications as well as looking attractive. The sloping sides not only make hedge cutting easier, but they also expose the whole surface of the hedge to sunlight, which helps to keep it growing well.

In colder areas, snowfall may be a problem, especially when the hedge is created from evergreen plants. Snow and ice accumulating on the top of the foliage can make the branches splay out or even break, causing considerable damage to the plants. A hedge with sloping sides is less likely to be affected.

When you clip a hedge, always start at the bottom and work upward, so that the clippings fall clear as they are cut rather than tangling up in the next area to be clipped. If you are using a mechanical hedge trimmer, you will find it easier to cut upward in a series of sweeping, arc-like actions, holding the cutting edge parallel to the hedge as you work.

Clipping and shaping

Once the hedge has reached its required height, regularly prune the top to about 12in (30cm) below this height. This will allow new, soft growth to hide any pruning cuts.

If you want a particular shape or profile, use a pre-cut wooden template. Draw your desired shape on the template, then cut it out with a saw. Place the template against or over the hedge so that you can easily shear or remove any growth that protrudes beyond the template. If you need to create a mirror image of the shape on the opposite side of the plant, flip the template over and use it to shape the other side. Once the profile has been established, you may find that you don't need to use the template every year.

The easiest way to level the top of a hedge is to stretch brightly colored garden twine along the hedge, supporting it on two posts to hold it taut at the appropriate height.

Clipping the sides In spring, starting at the bottom of the hedge, clip upward. Aim to cut the current season's growth back to a point just above the pruning cuts left by the previous trimming. Use hand pruners to remove any dead or dying leaves of shoots as you come across them.

Clipping the top Position two posts or stout canes about 12ft (4m) apart and just touching the front of the hedge. At the height desired, stretch some garden twine between the posts. Use brightly colored string so that you can see it clearly. Start clipping the top of the hedge, using hand pruners or long-handled pruners (loppers) for the thicker stems. Brush away any prunings and allow them to fall to the ground.

SHAPING
Use a template while clipping and training to create a particular hedge profile.

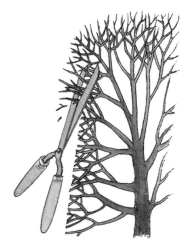

PRUNE UPWARD
Always clip from the bottom up toward the top of the hedge so that the trimmings fall away from the area being pruned.

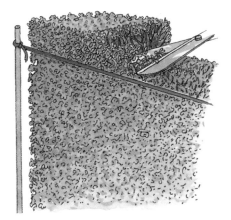

LEVEL TOP
Use a post and a brightly colored line as a guide to produce an even hedge top.

An overgrown hedge should be pruned in stages over several seasons.

FEEDING

Hedges are usually clipped several times a year, which diminishes the food reserves within the plants, and thereby reduces their growth rate. Adding an annual mulch of well-rotted garden compost or manure or applying a general fertilizer will help compensate. Feeding is particularly important after renovation pruning.

RENOVATION PRUNING

A hedge will eventually outgrow its intended space and may be damaged by strong winds or snow. Many plants used for hedging respond well to hard pruning for rejuvenation; when this succeeds it is often difficult to tell that the plants have actually been cut back hard. Don't forget that conifers, with the exception of *Taxus* spp. (yew) and *Thuja* spp. (arborvitae), cannot produce new growth from old wood and should never be renovation pruned.

When a hedge becomes seriously overgrown, staged remedial pruning, which is done over several seasons, is preferable to a single drastic pruning. If possible, always tackle the more sheltered side of the hedge first, because it will respond more quickly and help to protect the garden when the other side of the hedge is cut back.

Remedial pruning to reduce width

Year 1 In spring, cut all the lateral growth on one side of the hedge back to within about 6in (15cm) of the main stems. Trim the growth on the other side of the hedge as usual.

Year 2 The following spring, cut the growth on the other side of the hedge back to within about 6in (15cm) of the main stems. Lightly trim the new growth on the side of the hedge that was pruned severely in the previous year. At the same time, keep the top of the hedge in check by trimming the new growth lightly to encourage the shoots to branch further down the main stems.

TOOLS

Hand or power trimmers are normally used to trim hedges, but you may need to use hand pruners on larger-leaved evergreen plants, such as *Ilex* (holly) and *Aucuba* (Japanese laurel), even though it will take longer. On these types of hedges, mechanical trimmers will cut large leaves in half, causing unsightliness as they slowly turn yellow and die. You will need a stepladder or stable platform to cut a hedge more than 5ft (1.5m) high.

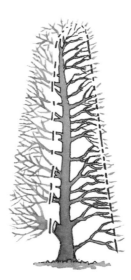

REMEDIAL PRUNING TO REDUCE WIDTH
Year 1: Cut one side of the hedge back hard, but trim the opposite side only lightly.

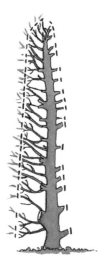

Year 2: Reverse the process, lightly trimming the new growth and cutting the older growth on the opposite side back hard.

Hedges and topiary plants
will help balance a garden
feature or vista, giving
definition and contrast.

Topiary shapes can be
created from popular
hedge plants by
trimming or clipping
them in the same way
as you would a hedge.

CLIMBERS

Climbers are usually grown as one-dimensional plants—that is, they are trained up and across a surface. They are pruned for the same reasons as other plants, but they may also need to be coaxed into growing toward and onto their supporting structure.

The aim is to achieve a well-spaced framework of shoots that grow close to their supports. This involves positioning and tying in the strongest stems. When you are pruning climbing plants, you must bear in mind the plant's habit of growth, no matter what genus it belongs to. A true climber will be self-supporting to some degree, which can affect its pruning and training.

Climbers that can cling to other plants or objects for support are quite different from the artificial category of wall shrubs (such as *Pyracantha*) that are specially trained to grow against a vertical surface. Some of these plants can be extremely vigorous, with shoots growing many feet each year, which often means that some wall shrubs need pruning twice a year to regulate growth and train the shoots.

Formative pruning with climbers often goes on throughout the life of the plant, not just when it is young (which is the case for most trees and shrubs). Climbing plants may also need to be pruned to prevent property

Campsis, a clinging vine, is best grown in a warm, sunny position where the warmth of the sun will mature the shoots that will provide next year's flowers.

damage. Some are pruned in the summer to trim growth from around doors and windows. Climbers that attach themselves to supports with sucker pads or aerial roots can do considerable structural damage if they are left unpruned.

Climbing plants fall into three broad categories according to their method of support.

CLINGERS

There are two main types of clinging vines. The first group includes natural clingers, such as the trumpet vine (*Campsis* spp.), English ivy (*Hedera helix*), and climbing hydrangea (*Hydrangea anomala* subsp. *petiolaris*), which support themselves by aerial roots. The second group is made up of plants such as Boston ivy (*Parthenocissus tricuspidata*) that cling with small sucker pads and usually need no additional support.

TWINERS

Twining plants are of three main types. Vines such as chocolate vine (*Akebia quinata*), climbing honeysuckles (*Lonicera* spp.), Russian vine (*Fallopia baldschuanica*), and wisteria support themselves by twining their stems around anything they can reach. Plants with twining leaf stalks, including the clematis (*Clematis* spp.) and *Smilax aspera*, grip other plants and objects. Plants with tendrils coil around any support they can reach and continue to coil to draw themselves closer to their supporting structure. This group includes grape vine (*Vitis* spp.) and passionflower (*Passiflora* spp.).

Wisteria has twining stems that will attach themselves to any other plants or structures for support in order to reach bright sunlight.

SCRAMBLERS

Some types of roses are called climbers but are in reality scramblers. They have rapidly growing stems that scramble through other plants and use hooked thorns to keep from sliding off their support. This is why the tip of each thorn usually angles back down the stem.

It is worth remembering that climbing sorts of bush roses (that is, roses with the word "climbing" before the cultivar name—'Climbing Iceberg', for example) may revert to their original bush form if they are severely pruned in the first two years after planting.

GROUNDCOVER

Planting low-growing, spreading plants to provide groundcover is a way of exploiting a plant's natural habit of growth to cover the soil. This has the dual advantages of looking attractive and suppressing weeds by preventing sunlight from reaching the soil.

Groundcover plants are usually those that grow no more than 18in (45cm) high but that spread outward. Your goal is to create a multistemmed plant that covers the soil with a network of lateral and sublateral branches and spreads out to block out light. This means that formative pruning is important because it will create a plant that is pruned frequently to induce the maximum number of sideshoots.

FORMATIVE PRUNING

Prune to encourage the development of a multistemmed plant with a framework of low, spreading, evenly spaced shoots close to ground level. In the first spring after planting, remove any dead or damaged shoots. Cut the remaining stems back to 6–8in (15–20cm) in length. Because these stems produce lateral branches, allow them to reach a length of 6–8in (15–20cm) before you cut out the tip of each shoot to encourage a more branching habit.

ROUTINE PRUNING

Established plants need little in the way of routine pruning and will continue to flower and fruit for many years without any pruning at all. However, as new growth forms on top of the old, plants gradually get higher and leave gaps beneath. As long as you are not dealing with a conifer (see page 160), pruning back to older wood every five or six years will reduce the height of the plants and stimulate new growth from the base, encouraging a dense carpet of growth.

Cut the plants down to within 6–8in (15–20cm) of soil level. Old or nonproductive shoots can be cut down to 2–3in (5–7cm) above ground level to encourage new shoots to grow as replacements.

REMEDIAL PRUNING

Plants sometimes grow beyond their allotted area. When this happens, avoid the common error of simply cutting the shoots back to a point along the edge of the bed or border. A better approach is to cut each encroaching stem back to a point where it will take the plant a full growing season to reach the edge of the bed again. Cut the shoots back to a bud or pair of buds and trim back any untidy growths. Remove any dead or damaged shoots.

Formative pruning is very important for groundcover plants, like this ivy, to encourage the development of a spreading, multistemmed plant.

As groundcover plants grow higher, they will leave gaps beneath. Stimulate new growth from the base by pruning the plants back every five or six years.

A dense thicket of *Erica carnea*. Such an abundance of shoots has been created by frequent pruning.

LOW-MAINTENANCE PRUNING

It is possible to minimize the amount of pruning you do in your garden, but this should be part of a thorough garden and plant management policy rather than a form of benign neglect. Plants need some pruning even in extremely low-maintenance gardens.

The low-maintenance approach to gardening has been used for many years in continental Europe to prune shrubs in municipal plantings. For a number of years, gardeners at the Royal National Rose Society trial grounds at St. Albans in England tried different pruning techniques on roses to see how the plants respond to different regimens. One of these schemes was to move away from the usual and long-established technique of using hand pruners, long-handled pruners (loppers), and pruning saws and instead to use garden shears or even mechanical hedge trimmers to prune bush roses. This method of

pruning involves cutting back all the plant stems to a predetermined height, regardless of the thickness of the stems or their position on the plants. It was found to produce larger numbers of good-quality flowers, although they were, on average, slightly smaller than those produced on plants pruned by traditional methods. It also appears to be particularly useful for plants growing in massed beds, where they can all be treated in the same way and retain some degree of uniformity.

It is important that all the prunings created from this method are removed and disposed of and that the cutting

tools are particularly sharp to ensure good, clean cuts with no snags or tears. (This, of course, is true with any other form of pruning.) Perhaps the main drawback is that it produces large quantities of small, sappy shoots, and this type of growth is susceptible to attack from pests and diseases—especially where the growth becomes congested.

A better approach seems to be a combination of traditional methods and power equipment. Prune plants with hedge trimmers for a period of four or five years and interrupt this with a year of hand pruning to thin out congested growth and dead wood.

LOW-MAINTENANCE PRUNING
It is possible to prune some bedding roses with a hedge trimmer, rather than with hand pruners.

After pruning, brush off all of the trimmings so that they fall onto the soil.

Gather up the prunings and dispose of them to reduce the spread of pests and diseases.

Many shrub roses will produce greater numbers of flowers using new low-maintenance pruning methods.

MINIMAL PRUNING
Remove only the oldest growths and allow the plant to develop naturally.

Use a gloved hand to stroke over the tops of the plants and brush off any trimmed shoots. Gather up and dispose of all the trimmings.

Another low-maintenance technique is to remove a set amount of growth. This normally involves removing complete shoots or branches every year or every other year to reduce the amount of pruning necessary. Often the shoots to be removed are selected on the basis of health and age. Dead, damaged, diseased, or dying growths are cut out first, followed by two or three of the oldest shoots, which are often removed with long-handled pruners (loppers) or a saw. This pruning method does not involve trimming, only removal of whole sections of the plant to create space for new growth.

MINIMAL PRUNING

In early spring or immediately after flowering, cut back two or three of the oldest stems as close to the ground as possible. This will give the maximum period of growth for the next season. Remove and dispose of the stems that have been pruned out. Take care that you do not damage the remaining growths when you remove the discarded stems.

For some plants, this method of pruning is not new at all but has been practiced for many years. Plants that produce lots of small, thin stems—heathers and lavenders, for example—have always been pruned with shears or clippers to trim off dead flowers as well as a small amount of stem growth. Many groundcover roses are also pruned in this way, and the old, spent flowers can be trimmed off with shears or mechanical trimmers.

First decide on the height at which the pruning cuts are to be made. Then use shears or a mechanical trimmer to cut off all the shoots standing above the predetermined height.

Your choice of plants can also play a part in the amount of pruning that needs to be done. Some plants do not need much regular pruning once they become established, especially if you have worked hard at the formative pruning when the specimens were first planted. Magnolias, camellias, most conifers, hebes, lilacs, rhododendrons, and skimmias will all do well for many years with an occasional light trim or deadheading to keep them tidy.

RENOVATION PRUNING

Left to their own devices, many plants flower and grow well for many years. After all, they seem to manage just fine when they are growing in the wild without a gardener in sight.

We choose most plants based on how they will look in our gardens, not how they would grow in the wild. Gardeners like to use their available space as well as possible, which means managing plants so they will perform in particular ways—produce flowers, fruit, or attractive foliage, or even, with a few plants, all of these things. However, most cultivated forms remain attractive only with regular attention. Untended plants often become tangled masses of old and new growth, and flowers gradually get smaller—especially after they start producing seeds regularly.

Plants may be neglected for a number of reasons. It may be that someone who has no interest in or aptitude for plants takes over a garden and finds the work too difficult or onerous. Or it may be that the gardener does not know how to prune the plants and decides to let them alone rather than risk harming them. Whatever the reason, the result is the same. But a plant will eventually have to be pruned if it is to remain a living garden specimen. This is when remedial or renovation pruning is necessary. Perhaps the hardest decision is whether the plant is actually worth the effort.

Some plants respond well to severe pruning and get a new lease on life, but others, such as *Cytisus* spp. (broom), will not survive as the stems dry and die back from pruning cuts. Most conifers, too, cannot produce new growth from old, bare wood. However, many trees and shrubs will respond to careful renovation pruning. Rather than pruning a plant severely in a single season, it is better to apply a phased pruning program over two or three years so the plant gradually replaces the old shoots. This will give you time to select the best of the new growths to train as replacements for main stems and laterals. Renovation pruning is best done in early spring.

GRAFTED PLANTS

Sometimes plants are budded or grafted—a named cultivar or variety is attached to a rootstock that has a quality, such as vigor or size, not found in the cultivar. Severe pruning to rejuvenate a grafted plant can lead to problems if a grafted plant is cut back too low. The cultivated variety on the top of the rootstock could be inadvertently removed altogether, or the rootstock may grow so vigorously that its sucker growths deny the choice selection the chance to grow.

Large shrubs, such as this *Photinia*, may need to be pruned in stages, rather than cutting all of the shoots back at the same time.

FEEDING

Every time a plant is pruned severely it should be fed. Apply a slow-release fertilizer or a mulch of well-rotted garden compost or manure to help the plant recover more quickly from the shock of the drastic pruning.

RECLAIMING AN OLD SHRUB

The first step is to remove all the dead, dying, diseased, and damaged wood. Do this while the plant is actively growing because it is much easier to tell what is healthy and what is not. Next, remove about half of the remaining live stems, cutting them down to ground level. Finally, cut all the sideshoots on the remaining stems back to within three or four buds of these main stems.

The following year, cut down all the stems that were trimmed but not cut out the previous year. You may need to thin new stems that have grown in the previous season to prevent overcrowding. Keep only the strongest, healthiest stems and make sure they are well placed to provide a good overall shape. Remove the

RENOVATING AN OLD, STRAGGLY PLANT
Cut all the stems back close to ground level to stimulate new growth.

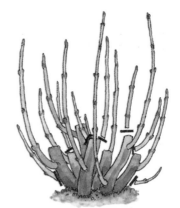

Select the strongest of the new shoots and allow them to grow. Remove any weaker shoots.

shoots you are not keeping, cutting out all thin, straggly, or damaged stems. Cut the unneeded stronger stems back to three or four buds, so that they can produce replacement growths if required.

With grafted plants, remove any suckering shoots emerging from the rootstock. If they originate from above soil level, rip off the stem by hand to remove all the dormant buds around their bases. If suckers emerge through the soil, dig the soil from around the base of the sucker and

pull the sucker away by hand; replace the soil after removing the sucker.

If the plant responds well to the rejuvenation program, within three to five years it should be impossible to tell how badly neglected the plant was beforehand. After rejuvenation pruning, watch the plants carefully—they often produce large amounts of soft, sappy growth susceptible to pests and diseases. Don't forget to remove woody stumps that remain after the plant starts to regrow. They could become sites of fungal rots.

CROWN LIFTING
This is a technique used to remove the lower branches from a tree in order to raise the crown.

CROWN THINNING
This reduces the density of the branches to allow more light into a garden or reduce the wind resistance of a large tree.

SPECIALIZED PRUNING

A number of pruning techniques are used only in special circumstances or to achieve a particular effect with, or result from, a plant. These special practices often replace routine pruning when it does not work as intended.

NICKING AND NOTCHING

Some plants naturally produce long sections of bare stem with hardly any branches, and you may occasionally need to correct the balance of the branch framework to improve its structure and overall appearance.

If you want to restrict the development of a bud or shoot, making a small, V-shaped nick with a sharp knife just below a bud can restrict the supply of growth-promoting chemicals and inhibit the growth of the shoot directly above it. Alternatively, if you want to encourage the development or growth of a particular bud, making a small

V-shaped notch just above it can increase its vigor and stimulate new growth. Notching can also stimulate the production of sideshoots on sections of bare stem.

This type of formative pruning is most effective in spring just as the new growth starts and when plants are growing vigorously as the sap starts to rise.

POLLARDING

Pollarding is a traditional method of hard pruning that gives a constant and renewable supply of shoots. It is especially useful for getting a plant to produce plenty of relatively thin,

one-year-old shoots rather than allowing it to produce a heavy framework of thick branches.

Pollarding involves pruning in spring either annually or biannually. Cut the existing branches down to within 2–3in (5–7cm) of the main stem, which can be up to 6ft (2m) above ground. Vigorous plants—such as poplar or cottonwood (*Populus* spp.), Indian bean tree (*Catalpa* spp.), linden (*Tilia* spp.), sycamore (*Platanus* spp.), redbud (*Cercis* spp.), and some willows (*Salix* cvs.)—can be pollarded to provide a display of attractive leaves or brightly colored young shoots in winter.

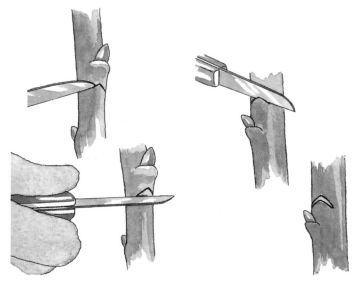

NICKING
Make a cut just below a bud to restrict its growth.

NOTCHING
Make a cut just above a bud to encourage its growth.

POLLARDING
Cut all the stems back to small stubs of growth very close to the main stem. As new growth develops, thin out the shoots so that only the thickest and strongest remain.

Above left: Many willows are grown for their brightly colored new bark and are therefore pollarded to encourage the development of fresh, new stems each spring.

Above right: Coppicing trees such as *Corylus* and *Sambucus* will stimulate the production of large, brightly colored leaves in the spring.

COPPICING

Coppicing—or stooling as it is also known—is one of the oldest pruning techniques. It was used as a method of woodland management for almost 700 years to produce young, straight stems for making fencing and material to supply charcoal burners. These days it is done to produce a particular type of growth and is restricted mainly to plants that can produce stems with brightly colored bark or those that bear attractive leaves.

The main aim is to produce vigorous stems with larger than normal leaves on plants such as princess tree (*Paulownia tomentosa*), smoke tree (*Cotinus coggygria*), elderberry (*Sambucus* spp.), gum tree (*Eucalyptus* spp.), hazel (*Corylus* spp.), and willow (*Salix* spp.). All these plants produce leaves that are brightly colored or otherwise decorative.

Alternatively, the technique can produce brightly colored stems on snakebark maples (*Acer davidii* and *A. pennsylvanicum*), dogwood (*Cornus* spp.), silver-stemmed bramble (*Rubus biflorus*), and white willow (*Salix alba*), all of which are most ornamental through winter after the leaves have fallen. The gum tree (*Eucalyptus* spp.) is also often coppiced to provide both stems and leaves for flower arrangers.

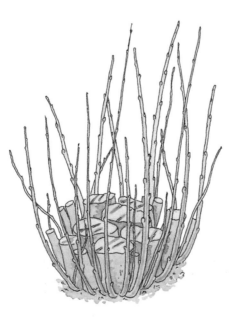

COPPICING
Cut all the stems back to small stubs of growth very close to ground level. As new growth develops, thin out the shoots so that only the thickest and strongest remain.

Right: Pleaching involves training the lateral shoots horizontally along wire supports.

Opposite page: An avenue of pleached trees is an attractive sight, particularly when the lateral shoots start to intertwine. The hedge-on-stilts effect created by a row of pleached trees in spring and summer is perfect for providing a formal setting, while still allowing light to reach the plants below.

PLEACHING

At first glance, a row of pleached trees looks like a hedge on legs or stilts. In years gone by, avenues of pleached trees were regarded as status symbols, and landowners in Tudor England would boast about how many gardeners they needed to maintain their pleached trees. Gardens in Europe, such as the royal gardens at the Palace of Versailles in France, originally contained numerous long avenues flanked by pleached trees. In recent years, the technique has become popular again, especially in formal gardens.

The process, which combines pruning and training, is extremely labor intensive and involved. Lateral shoots are trained horizontally along wire supports, and any shoots that branch out from these laterals are pruned back to within one or two buds of their point of origin. The lateral shoots are intertwined as they grow, so that they eventually form a screen. Once this framework is established, the shoots are clipped as they would be on an ordinary hedge.

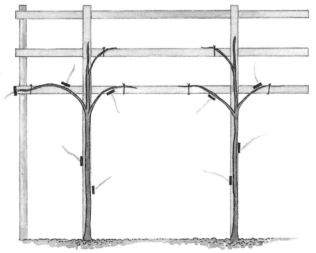

PLEACHING
Train the main stem into the supporting framework, remove any shoots forming on the main stem, and remove any lateral shoots that cannot be trained into the framework.

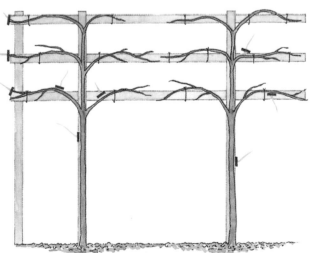

As the leader reaches the top of the supporting framework, begin to train it horizontally (train all the leaders in the same direction). Shorten any very long lateral shoots and remove any shoots forming on the main stem.

As the shoots from each tree reach each other, begin to weave them together. Cut back to a single bud any shoots growing at right angles to the main framework.

Festooning a tree involves training long, flexible shoots to curve inward toward the base of the plant to increase flower production.

FESTOONING

Many flowering plants tend to produce a greater number of flowers and, in some cases, more fruits when the shoots are growing horizontally or slightly below horizontal, so that the shoot tip is below the point where the lateral branch emerges from the main trunk. Some plants, such as crab apple (*Malus* spp.) and silver-leaved pear (*Pyrus salicifolia*), often produce long, flexible stems, which may take several years to produce flower-bearing spurs.

Rather than pruning back these long shoots and fighting against the natural growth habit of the plant—cutting them back will only stimulate the development of more, similar shoots to replace those you have removed—you can tie them down so that they form loops. Attach a length of string about 6in (15cm) from the end of a long shoot and loosely fasten the other end of the string to the base of the main stem to keep the stems in place. Bending the stems like this causes a redistribution of growth-promoting chemicals in the shoots, and the buds along these curving stems will develop and produce lateral shoots that can be pruned back to three to five buds in summer. They will form flower-bearing spurs the following year and flower the next spring. If these branches become overcrowded, a complete branch or section of a branch can be removed, leaving room for a replacement to develop.

ROOT PRUNING

This technique is rarely practiced these days, but it can be used as a last-ditch effort to control the vigor of plants or reduce root competition. It is also an excellent way of encouraging them to flower more frequently. If a plant is getting too big or producing too much shoot growth, you may be tempted to cut off the top of the plant, but this often simply makes it produce more

ROOT PRUNING
Dig a trench around the tree, just outside the spread of the canopy of branches. The trench should be one spade's width wide and about 18in (45cm) deep.

Saw through any thick roots uncovered by the trench and remove the loose ends completely before refilling the trench with soil.

vigorous shoots or creates a hopelessly misshapen plant.

If a plant is to produce healthy, balanced growth, there must be a physical and chemical balance between the shoots and the roots. Naturally occurring chemicals that originate in a plant's roots directly influence the rate of growth and the balance between shoot development and flower production. Root pruning works by removing sections of root that are responsible for producing these chemicals. Restricting their supply changes the balance of chemicals in a plant, which limits the development and extension growth of the branches and reduces a plant's tendency to produce flowers rather than shoots. One advantage is that root pruning encourages the plant to produce a more branched root system with a higher proportion of small, fibrous roots.

Root pruning does have a number of disadvantages, however, and the timing must be precise. It must be done in spring when the windiest weather of the year is over. If you remove large sections of major supporting roots in fall, the plant is likely to blow over in strong winter winds. In spring the healing process and formation of new roots will be rapid, if the plant is healthy enough to survive root pruning. Remember, too, that some plants are propagated by root cuttings, and if plants such as some locusts (*Robinia* spp.), sassafras (*Sassafras albium*), glory flower (*Clerodendrum* spp.), and poplars (*Populus* spp.) are root pruned and the sections of severed root are left in the ground, they may start to produce shoots and quickly colonize large areas of the garden.

BARK RINGING

This is a simple but effective technique for restricting a plant's growth if other pruning methods have not had the desired effect. It can also be used when root pruning is impractical—if the main roots are located under a path or driveway, for example.

In midspring, remove a narrow strip of bark, ¼–½in (6–12mm) wide, from around the main trunk. Take care that you don't form a complete ring around the trunk or you will kill the plant. The depth of the cut is important. You need to cut down to the cambium layer, the thin layer of cells on the surface of the wood, immediately below the bark. Removing this strip of bark forms a barrier that restricts the downward movement of the carbohydrates manufactured in the leaves and growth-promoting chemicals, and they will accumulate in the stem just above the ring. This starves the plant of food and growth-promoting chemicals in the area below the ring. The root system is below the ring, and root activity is slowed down, which checks the top-growth.

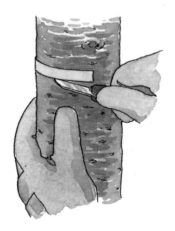

BARK RINGING
Wrap a piece of tape around the stem of the tree as a guide.

Cut through the bark on each side of the tape, leaving a small segment of bark in place. Lift out the remaining strip of bark around the stem.

Cover the cut surface with a strip of electrician's adhesive insulation tape.

When to prune most species

PLANT	PRUNING TIME
Abelia	Early or late spring
Actinidia	Late winter or early spring
Amelanchier	Late spring
Aucuba japonica	Midspring
Berberis (deciduous)	Early summer
Berberis (evergreen)	Early summer
Bougainvillea	Early spring
Buddleja	Early or midspring
Callicarpa	Midspring
Callistemon	Late summer
Calluna	Late winter or early spring
Camellia	Midspring
Ceanothus (deciduous)	Early or midspring
Ceanothus (evergreen)	Early spring or midsummer
Cercis	Early summer
Chaenomeles	Late spring or early summer
Choisya	Late spring
Clematis (early-flowering)	Late spring or early summer
Clematis (midseason-flowering)	Late winter or early spring
Clematis (late-flowering)	Late winter or early spring
Cornus alba and Cornus sericea	Early or midspring
Cotinus	Early spring
Cotoneaster (deciduous)	Late winter
Cotoneaster (evergreen)	Winter or midspring
Ficus	Late winter or early spring
Forsythia	Late spring or early summer
Fremontodendron	Midsummer
Fuchsia	Early spring
Hedera	Early spring
Hibiscus	Late winter or early spring
Hydrangea (shrub)	Early spring
Hydrangea (climber)	Late summer

PLANT	PRUNING TIME
Ilex	Mid- or late summer
Jasminum	Early spring
Lagerstroemia	Early spring
Lavandula	Early to midspring or late summer
Lonicera (climber)	Late summer
Lonicera (shrub)	Late spring or early summer
Magnolia	Midsummer
Mahonia	Early or midspring
Malus	Mid- or late summer
Osmanthus	Late spring
Passiflora	Early spring
Philadelphus	Late summer
Potentilla	Midspring
Prunus (deciduous)	Late spring
Prunus (evergreen)	Late winter
Pyracantha	Late spring and late summer
Rhododendron	Midsummer
Rosa (large-flowered)	Late winter or early spring
Rosa (cluster-flowered)	Late winter or early spring
Rosa (shrub and species)	Late winter or early spring
Rosa (climbers)	Early or mid-fall
Rosa (ramblers)	Early or mid-fall
Rosmarinus	Late summer
Salix	Early or midspring
Sambucus	Winter
Spiraea	Early summer
Syringa	Midsummer
Taxus	Mid- or late spring
Vaccinium	Late winter
Viburnum (deciduous)	Late winter
Viburnum (evergreen)	Early or midsummer
Vitis	Late winter
Weigela	Midsummer
Wisteria	Late winter and midsummer

No- or low-prune plants

DECIDUOUS	DECIDUOUS	EVERGREEN	EVERGREEN
Acer palmatum and cvs.	Hydrangea anomala subsp. petiolaris	Aucuba japonica and cvs.	Ilex opaca and Ilex aquifolium and cvs.
Cercis spp. and cvs.	Ilex verticillata	Camellia spp. and cvs.	Osmanthus spp. and cvs.
Chaenomeles spp. and cvs.	Magnolia spp. and cvs.	Choisya ternata and cvs.	Photinia ×fraseri and cvs.
Cotinus coggygria and cvs.	Rhododendron spp. and cvs.	Cistus ×corbariensis	Prunus spp. and cvs.
Cotoneaster upright spp. and cvs.	Syringa spp. and cvs.	Cotoneaster upright spp. and cvs.	Rhododendron spp. and cvs.
Daphne spp. and cvs.		Euonymus spp. and cvs.	Tsuga spp. and cvs.
Hibiscus syriacus and cvs.		Gaultheria mucronata and cvs.	Viburnum spp. and cvs.

Suitable hedging plants

FORMAL HEDGES (CLIPPED)				
PLANT	EVERGREEN/ DECIDUOUS	BEST HEIGHT	HEDGE PRUNING TIMES	RESPONDS TO REMEDIAL PRUNING
Buxus sempervirens	E	1–3ft (30cm–1m)	Once in spring and twice in summer (but never in winter)	Yes
Carpinus betulus	D	5–20ft (1.5–6m)	Once in late summer	Yes
Chamaecyparis lawsoniana	E	4–8ft (1.2–2.4m)	Once in late spring, once in early fall	No
Crataegus monogyna	D	5–10ft (1.5–3m)	Once in summer, once in fall	Yes
×Cupressocyparis leylandii	E	6½–20ft (2–6m)	Once in spring and twice in summer (but never in winter)	No
Elaeagnus ×ebbingei	E	5–10ft (1.5–3m)	Once in mid- to late summer	Yes
Escallonia spp.	E	4–8ft (1.2–2.4m)	Once immediately after flowering	Yes
Euonymus fortunei	E	4–6ft (1.2–2m)	Once in summer	Yes
Fagus sylvatica	D	5–20ft (1.5–6m)	Once in late summer	Yes
Griselinia littoralis	E	4–10ft (1.2–3m)	Once in late spring, once in late summer	No
Ilex hybrids and cvs.	E	4–13ft (1.2–4m)	Once in late summer	Yes
Ligustrum spp.	D	5–10ft (1.5–3m)	Once in spring and twice in summer (but never in winter)	No
Lonicera nitida	E	3–4ft (1–1.2m)	Once in spring and twice in summer (but never in winter)	No
Osmanthus spp.	E	6–10ft (2–3m)	Once in spring	Yes
Prunus laurocerasus	E	4–10ft (1.2–3m)	Once in late winter	Yes
Pyracantha spp.	E	6½–10ft (2–3m)	Once after flowering, once in late summer (but avoid pruning berries)	No
Taxus baccata	E	4–20ft (1.2–6m)	Once in summer, once in fall	No
Thuja spp.	E	5–20ft (1.5–6m)	Once in late spring, once in early fall	No

INFORMAL HEDGES (UNCLIPPED)				
PLANT	EVERGREEN/ DECIDUOUS	BEST HEIGHT	HEDGE PRUNING TIMES	RESPONDS TO REMEDIAL PRUNING
Berberis darwinii	E	5–8ft (1.5–2.4m)	Once after flowering	Yes
Berberis thunbergii	D	2–4ft (60cm–1.2m)	Once after flowering	Yes
Choisya ternata	E	6–8ft (2–2.4m)	Once after flowering	Yes
Cotoneaster lacteus	E	5–7ft (1.5–1.2m)	Once after fruiting	Yes
Crataegus monogyna	D	5–10ft (1.5–3m)	Once in winter	Yes
Escallonia spp.	E	4–8ft (1.2–2.4m)	Once immediately after flowering	Yes
Forsythia ×intermedia	D	5–8ft (1.5–2.4m)	Once after flowering	Yes
Fuchsia magellanica	D	3–5ft (1–1.5m)	Once in spring, to remove old stems	Yes
Garrya elliptica	E	5–7ft (1.5–1.2m)	Once immediately after flowering	No
Hibiscus syriacus	D	6–10ft (2–3m)	Once in spring	No
Ilex aquifolium and *Ilex opaca*	E	6½–20ft (2–6m)	Once in late summer	Yes
Lavandula spp.	E	1–3ft (30cm–1m)	Once in spring, once after flowering	No
Pyracantha spp.	E	6½–10ft (2–3m)	Once after flowering, once in fall (but avoid pruning berries)	No
Rosa rugosa	D	3¼–5ft (1–1.5m)	Once in spring, to remove old stems	Yes
Viburnum spp.	E	3¼–8ft (1–2m)	Once after flowering	No

GLOSSARY

Alternate (buds/leaves) Leaves that occur at different levels on opposite sides of the stem.

Apex The tip of a shoot, from which extension growth is made.

Apical bud The uppermost bud in the growing point of a stem (also known as the terminal bud).

Axil The angle at the point where the leaf or branch joins the main stem of a plant.

Axillary bud A bud that occurs in the leaf axil.

Bark A protective layer of cells on the outer surface of the roots and stems of woody plants.

Bark ringing The practice of removing a ring of bark from the trunk of a tree to help control vigor.

Biennial bearing A plant that slips into a habit of producing fruit on a two-year cycle.

Bleeding The excessive flow of sap from spring-pruned plants.

Blind bud A bud that fails to produce a terminal bud.

Branch A lateral part growing from the main trunk/stem of a tree/shrub.

Break A shoot growing from a bud as a result of pruning.

Broad-leaved Deciduous or evergreen plants with flat, broad leaves.

Bud A condensed shoot containing an embryonic shoot or flower.

Bud union The point where a cultivar is budded onto a rootstock.

Bush A multi-branched plant with a number of branches of similar size.

Callus The plant tissue that forms as a protective cover over a cut or wounded surface.

Climber A self-supporting plant capable of growing vertically.

Compound leaf A leaf consisting of a number of small segments (leaflets).

Conifer A classification of plants that have naked ovules often borne in cones, and narrow, needlelike foliage.

Coppicing The severe pruning of plants to ground level on an annual basis.

Cordon A tree trained to produce fruiting spurs from a main stem.

Crotch The place where two branches or stems join or where a branch meets a trunk.

Crown The upper branches and foliage of a tree.

Cultivar A plant form that originated in cultivation rather than having been found in the wild.

Deadheading The deliberate removal of dead flowerheads or seed-bearing fruits.

Deciduous Plants that produce new leaves in the spring and shed them in the fall.

Dieback The death of plant growth downward from the shoot tip.

Dormant period A period of reduced growth through the winter.

Espalier A tree trained to produce several horizontal tiers of branches from a vertical main stem.

Evergreen Plants that retain their actively growing leaves through the winter.

Framework The main permanent branch structure of a woody plant.

Fruit The seed-bearing vessel on a plant.

Graft union The point where a cultivar is grafted onto a rootstock.

Grafting A propagation method involving the joining of two or more separate plants together.

Hybrid A cross between two or more species or forms of a species.

Lateral A sideshoot arising from an axillary bud.

Leader The main dominant shoot or stem of the plant (usually the terminal shoot).

Leaf The main lateral organ of a green plant.

Leaflet One of the small segments of a compound leaf.

Loppers Long-handled pruners used for pruning thicker branches.

Maiden A young (one-year-old) budded or grafted tree.

Mulch A layer of material applied to cover the soil.

Opposite Where leaves, buds, or stems are arranged in pairs directly opposite one another.

Ornamentals Plants grown primarily for their decorative value rather than commercial usefulness or for crops.

Perianth The two outer whorls (calyx and corolla or sepals and petals) that first protect and then display the generative parts. In general, perianth is used when the petals and sepals look alike, as in a tulip.

Pinching out The removal (usually with finger and thumb) of a shoot's growing point to encourage the development of lateral shoots.

Pollarding The severe pruning of a tree's main branches back to the main stem or trunk.

Rambler A vigorous trailing plant with a scrambling habit.

Renewal pruning A pruning system based on the systematic replacement of lateral fruiting branches.

Root The underground support system of a plant.

Root ball The root system and surrounding soil/compost of a plant.

Root pruning The cutting of live plant roots to control the vigor of a plant.

Rootstock The root system onto which a cultivar is budded or grafted.

Sap The juice or blood of a plant.

Scion The propagation material taken from a cultivar or variety to be used for budding or grafting.

Shoot A branch stem or twig.

Sideshoot A stem arising from a branch stem or twig.

Spur A short fruit/flower-bearing branch.

Standard A tree with a clear stem of at least 6ft (2m).

Stem The main shoot of a tree.

Stone fruits A term usually reserved for fruit-bearing members of the genus *Prunus*, e.g., apricot, cherry, damson, plum.

Stooling The severe pruning of plants to within 4–6in (10–15cm) of ground level on an annual basis.

Sublateral A sideshoot arising from an axillary bud of a lateral shoot.

Sucker A shoot arising from below ground level.

Tap root The large main root of a plant.

Tendril A modified stem or leaf that twines around supports, enabling the plant to climb.

Tepal A division of a perianth.

Terminal bud The uppermost bud in the growing point of a stem (also known as the apical bud).

Thinning The removal of branches to improve the quality of those remaining.

Topiary The imposition of an artificial shape, geometric or representational, on a tree or shrub by trimming and training.

Tree A woody perennial plant usually consisting of a clear stem or trunk and a framework or head of branches.

Trunk The main stem of a mature tree.

Union (graft union) The point where a cultivar is grafted onto a rootstock.

Variegated Plant parts (usually leaves) marked with a blotched irregular pattern of colors, such as gold or silver on a base color of green.

Vegetative growth Nonflowering stem growth.

Whip A young one-year-old tree with no lateral branches.

Whorl The arrangement of three or more leaves, buds, or shoots arising from the same level.

Wood The lignified tissue of trees and shrubs but sometimes used as a synonym for growth.

Wound Any cut or damaged area on a plant.

INDEX

CREDITS

We would like to thank and acknowledge the following for supplying images reproduced in this book:

Key: l (left), r (right), a (above), b (below)

www.shutterstock.com: p.1 (leaves, also on pp.3, 5, 17, 153) Bariskina; p.2 iMoved Studio; p.4 Nataliia Melnychuk; p.6 Oleksandr Chub; p.8a Andrew Fletcher; p.8b Vladimir Zhupanenko; p.9 GryT; p.12ar encierro; p.13ar Bachkova Natalia; p.14 Delpixel; p.15a Deatonphotos; p.15b Jason Kolenda; pp.16–17 Michele Paccione; p.18 Isabel Sala Casteras; p.20 mizy; p.22 Dudakova Elena; p.24 zvetok; p.26 Oleg1824; p.28 EMFA16; p.30 Y. Raewongkhot; p.32 Vahan Abrahamyan; p.34 Radka Palenikova; p.36 Inna Reznik; p.38 Greta Nurk; p.40 MaryAbramkina; p.42 Svetlana Mahovskaya; p.44 Juriaan Wossink; p.46 guentermanaus; p.48 Lev Savitskiy; p.50 Gurcharan Singh; p.52 Mali lucky; p.54 Mariusz S. Jurgielewicz; p.56 Garmasheva Natalia; p.58 Flojke; p.60 Kateryna_Moroz; p.62 Agnes Kantaruk; p.64 Craig Russell; p.66 Evgeny Gubenko; p.68 Nick Pecker; p.70 AlessandraRC; p.72 Nawin nachiangmai; p.74 villorejo; p.76 LensTravel; p.78 aoya; p.80 Flegere; p.82 nnattalli; p.84 pisitpong2017; p.86 ananaline; p.88 Iva Vagnerova; p.90 JurateBuiviene; p.92 Bo Starch; p.94 george photo cm; p.96 APugach; p.98 nnattalli; p.100 Zhao jian kang; p.102 Lars Ove Jonsson; p.104 Sergey; p.106 photowind; p.108 joe yasuoka; p.110 flaviano fabrizi; p.112 dadalia; p.114 Grisha Bruev; p.116 Stella Oriente; p.118 Paul Atkinson; p.120 Nick Pecker; p.122 Motoko; p.124 Monika Pa; p.126 Maren Winter; p.128 Andrew Fletcher; p.130 SGr; p.132 Vikulin; p.134 loflo69; p.136 Mariusz S. Jurgielewicz; p.138 Studio Barcelona; p.140 Robert Biedermann; p.142 EMFA16; p.144 hfuchs; p.146 Magdalenagalkiewicz; p.148 nnattalli; pp.152–153 allstars; p.155a Peter Turner Photography; p.157a Andrew Mayovskyy; p.159a Chrislofotos; p.159b Jeanie333; p.162a Artush; p.162b photowind; p.164 North Devon Photography; p.165 Monika Pa; p.168a Thomas Soellner; p.169a Yolanta; p.169b PA; p.170 nadtochiy; p.171 Kristina Bessolova; p.172 Svetlana Mahovskaya; p.173a ESB Basic; p.173b Freekee; p.175a LiliGraphie; p.176 Philip Bird LRPS CPAGB; p.179al RockerStocker; p.179ar Deatonphotos; p.180a Martin Kemp; p.181a Germanova Antonina; p.182a Peter Turner Photography.

All other illustrations and photographs are the copyright of Quarto Publishing plc. While every effort has been made to credit contributors, Quarto would like to apologize should there have been any omissions or errors—and would be pleased to make the appropriate correction for future editions of the book.